WHO KILLED
BRITISH CINEMA?

Vinod Mahindru
& Jonathan Gems

QUOTA FILMS

First published in Great Britain 2017

QUOTA FILMS LTD
49, Skyline, 165 Granville Street, Birmingham B1 1JW

The rights of Vinod Mahindru and Jonathan Gems to be identified as the Authors of the Work have been asserted by them in accordance with Section 7 of the Copyright, Designs and Patents Act 1988.

ISBN 978-1-9998422-0-8

A CIP record for this book is available from the British Library.

Quota Films is committed to a sustainable future, in accordance with the United Nations global agenda for sustainable development. We use approved materials that are natural, renewable, recyclable and sustainable from wood grown in forests that conform to international logging and environmental standards and are processed in accordance with the American National Standard for Information Sciences - Permanence of Paper for Printed Library Materials (ANSI Z39.48-1992)

www.whokilledbritishcinema.com

PRINTED AND BOUND BY IMPRINTDIGITAL.COM
Formatted by The Artful Bookman

Cover by: Tristan
Back cover film still: 'Carry on Camping' (1969) Directed by Gerald Thomas
© Rank Film Distributors of America/Photofest

CONTENTS

PREFACE

I first met Vinod Mahindru and Robin Dutta when they came to interview me for a documentary they were making about the British film industry.

I liked what they were trying to do, and enjoyed the finished product, which they screened at the Prince Charles Cinema, just off Leicester Square, in London.

Vinod told me he was planning a book to accompany the film and, later, sent me his first draft, asking for comments.

This led to me collaborating with him and examining, in a little more depth, what he and Robin Dutta had explored and exposed in their film 'Who Killed British Cinema?'

I think a lot of people are tired of the lies trotted out about British films. This book is an attempt to set the record straight.

Some of it may surprise you.

Jonathan Gems

INTRODUCTION

In July, 2002, we were in despair.

Since we were kids, my friend, Robin Dutta, and I had always wanted to make movies. We'd both done film courses and made short films, but there seemed to be no way to break into features.

Then, in 2002, Channel Four's *Film4* closed down. It was like the end of the world. Who could we go to now with our film projects?

Well, there was the BBC, which part-financed five films a year; Nik Powell's *Scala Productions*, which made two films a year; and the British arm of the French film studio *Pathé*, which made one film a year. And Pathé was the only company that could guarantee a theatrical release.

British Cinema was just about dead.

Yet, unaccountably, our government ministers, the UK Film Council, the British Film Institute, BAFTA,[1] and our print and broadcast media never stopped gushing about the 'success' of British films.

This made no sense at all.

We decided to investigate, and do a documentary about it. We called the documentary: *Who Killed British Cinema?*

This book is its companion piece.

Vinod Mahindru

---

[1] British Academy of Film & Television Arts

Chapter One
A LITTLE BACKGROUND

"We learn from history."

John Lennon

Who invented the movies? The first movie camera was patented in 1876 by an English gentleman named Wordsworth Donisthorpe.

In 1878, another English gentleman - Eadweard Muybridge - made the first moving picture: *The Horse in Motion* – although he didn't use a movie camera, but multiple still cameras.

Ten years later, in 1888, a naturalized Englishman, named Louis Le Prince, who lived in Leeds, invented a movie camera and made short films on sensitized paper. In the same year, in Bristol, William Friese-Greene, made short films on celluloid.

The first American film wasn't made until 1890. The first French film (of workers leaving the Lumière factory) wasn't made until 1895. Yet, both the French and Americans claim they invented Cinema. They didn't.

We did.

In 1895, the great English film pioneer, Robert Paul, patented a new 35mm camera and film projector, and shot *Incident at Clovelly Cottage* and *Cricketer Jumping Over A Garden Gate* – and, in 1896, he made the first-ever fiction film: *The Arrest of a Pickpocket*. He followed this up, in the same year, with *A Soldier's Courtship*, starring Fred Storey – a well-known stage actor.

Robert Paul (known as the 'Father of British Cinema') built the first-ever movie production studio, with a laboratory able to process 8,000 feet of film a day.

Also, in 1896, while Léon Gaumont was developing a camera/projector in France – a British optician named Alfred Wrench, patented a camera/projector he called a *Cinematograph* (from which we get the word 'Cinema'), and used it, in 1897, to film Queen Victoria's Diamond Jubilee.

Moving pictures were shown at fairs, amusement arcades, and in music halls, and became so popular that, by 1912, there were more than thirty British studios financing, producing and distributing 'movies' throughout the world.

After the First World War, their popularity grew and grew. This was when the upper class regarded 'flickers' as a trivial, low-class novelty. People of quality went to the theatre, not the cinematograph. But the common people were mad about the 'flicks' so, in 1916, the government imposed an Entertainment Tax of 25% on the price of each cinema ticket.[2]

Despite this tax, British Cinema flourished and, by 1920, every week saw the release of three new motion pictures.

Unfortunately, Hollywood, with its bigger talent pool and greater capital investment, began beating out the home product and, by 1927, American films had seized 80% of our domestic market.

The government's response was to defend British Cinema by passing the *Cinematograph Films Act*, which introduced a 7.5% film quota.

---

[2] Over the following years, this tax went up and down. In some years, it went as high as 40%. In 1945, when the gross box office receipts of Britain's cinemas were £115million, the Treasury took £41million. Many campaigned against the Entertainment Tax and, in 1949, J. Arthur Rank threatened to stop making movies unless it was reduced. It *was* reduced but continued until 1957, when it was finally abolished.

7.5% of the UK market was ring-fenced for British films.

"The Act's supporters believed that by creating an artificial market for British films, increased economic activity in the production sector would lead to the growth of a self-sustaining industry."

WIKIPEDIA.

Hollywood's revenge was to boost the popularity of American films by setting up British subsidiaries of American companies to make bad British films. But despite these 'quota quickies' being despised by the public, they didn't kill British Cinema. In fact, they helped train future British directors, actors, and film technicians.

The film quota was so helpful to the British film industry that, by 1930, British films were commanding almost half the UK market. And investors were lining up to put their money into British film studios.

One of these was *British International Pictures*, which built the sound stages at Elstree.

John Maxwell, (the founder of *British International*) and his manager, John Grossman, made the first British talkie – *Blackmail*, directed by Alfred Hitchcock.[3]

Another studio that benefited from the quota was *British Lion*, founded in 1927 by Sam Smith. Between 1928 and 1973, *British Lion* financed, produced and distributed over a thousand movies.

In 1932, Alexander Korda, came to London and set up *London Films*.

---

[3] Some say the first British talkie was *The Clue of the New Pin* (1929) based on an Edgar Wallace novel, made by *British Lion*.

Korda, a Hungarian, was worried because he didn't know what kind of movies the natives liked. The story goes that, one day, in the back of a taxi, he asked the driver what would be a good subject for a film.

The cabdriver said: "Henry the Eighth."

"Why Henry the Eighth?"

"Because," grinned the cabbie, "He had six wives!"

Korda's first film - *The Private Life of Henry VIII* - starring Charles Laughton, came out in 1933, was a smash hit, and made him a fortune.

"During the 1930s, London Films, with its Big Ben logo, became associated with glossy but intelligent films, like the enjoyable comedy *The Ghost Goes West* (d. René Clair, 1935), the H.G. Wells scripted *Things to Come* (d. William Cameron Menzies, 1936), a spectacular science-fiction story with a strong anti-war message, or the Russian Revolution love story *Knight Without Armour* (d. Jacques Feyder, 1937), for which Korda managed to lure Hollywood megastar Marlene Dietrich for her only British role. His eye for talent led to him spotting the young Michael Powell and bringing him to London Films, where he united him with the Hungarian screenwriter Emeric Pressburger for *Spy in Black* (1939), creating perhaps British cinema's most illustrious partnership. He continued to direct himself, most impressively in the biopic *Rembrandt* (1936), in which he elicited a superb performance from Charles Laughton as the troubled, misunderstood Dutch painter."

Mark Duguid
BFI SCREEN ONLINE

In 1936 - three years after Korda started *London Films* – a devout Methodist named J. Arthur Rank, who was upset by the immoral values promoted in Hollywood films, set up Britain's biggest movie studio: *The Rank Organisation.*

At first, Arthur Rank was blocked by Hollywood's majority control of UK cinemas. Then, like today, most of our cinemas were owned or controlled by American corporations. Arthur Rank couldn't get his films released. Fortunately, he had rich friends - Christians like himself - who got together and helped him buy the *Gaumont* cinema chain (251 cinemas.)

Later, in 1942 - after building Pinewood Studios on an estate in Buckinghamshire - Rank bought the *Paramount* cinema chain, which brought his stock of movie theatres up to 619.

The *Cinematograph Films Act* of 1927 had a ten-year lifespan. So, in 1937, the Act was reviewed under the chairmanship of Lord Moyne. Its undoubted success encouraged Lord Moyne to retain the Act's provisions and increase the quota to 12.5%.

This further improved the fortunes of the British film industry, and *The Rank Organisation* grew into a replica of a major Hollywood studio, with a story department, art department, costume department, in-house training for actors, and seven-year contracts.

After the Second World War, in response to renewed competition from Hollywood, the government upped the film quota to 30% and formed the *National Film Finance Corporation* to provide capital for marketing and distribution.

It also introduced the *Eady Levy* to help film producers.

The Eady Levy, named after the Treasury official who devised it, added a 5% surcharge to every cinema ticket sold in

Britain. Cinema managers sent this surcharge to a central fund from which it was distributed to British producers.

American producers couldn't receive Eady money, so it was a way of getting Hollywood to pay 5% of its gross revenues as the price of admission to the UK market.[4]

By 1955 – with the help of the quota, the NFFC and the Eady Levy - over 100 British films were being released each year - a level not seen since the peak of 1920.

This was the "golden age of British Cinema," which produced masterworks such as *Brief Encounter, The Lady Vanishes, Great Expectations, In Which We Serve, The History of Mr. Polly, The Red Shoes, Doctor In the House, The Dam Busters*, Laurence Olivier's *Hamlet*, and *Henry V, Odd Man Out, The Browning Version, The Third Man, Oliver Twist, Life With the Lyons, Kind Hearts and Coronets, The Ladykillers,* and many more.

Then came television.

Television became a force in 1952 with the transmission of Queen Elizabeth's coronation, which attracted a huge audience.

By 1957, almost 20 million were watching TV for an average of two hours a night.

Many thought Cinema was doomed. Why pay to see a film and newsreels when you could watch shows and news at home for free?

Associated British Pictures and *The Rank Organisation* both decided to diversify.

When, in 1955, the government offered TV station contracts, *Associated British Pictures* bought a licence to broadcast to the

---

[4] It didn't take long for the Americans to outwit this tax by setting up British production companies that were wholly owned by Hollywood.

Midlands and the North - and set up *ABC-TV*. *Rank* bought the licence for Southern England, and set up *Southern Television.*

But, even though they bought into television, the British film studios continued to compete against television with colour film, Cinerama (widescreen), and movies in 3-D.

Television managements, which had a tough job filling each night with fresh content, begged the studios (some of which were their parent companies) to sell them their old films. But the studios refused. TV was the enemy!

It took a long time before people woke up to the realisation that TV could *promote* cinema-going.

Maddeningly, British Cinema's decline happened just as a new generation of outstanding filmmakers appeared: writers like Alun Owen, David Mercer, Norman Hudis, Charles Wood, Peter Barnes, Paul Mayersberg, Talbot Rothwell, Sheila Delaney, Robert Bolt, and Ruth Prawer Jhabvala (who wrote the *Merchant Ivory* films.) And directors like Lindsay Anderson, Tony Richardson, Jack Clayton, Mike Hodges, Ken Loach, Ken Russell, John Schlesinger, Alan Parker, Nicholas Roeg, James Ivory, Freddie Francis, and John Boorman.

The new crop of British actors was equally good: Peter O'Toole, Vanessa Redgrave, Albert Finney, Michael Caine, Richard Harris, Peter Sellers, Richard Burton, Sean Connery, Tom Courtenay, Diana Rigg, Robert Shaw, Alan Bates, Glenda Jackson, Terence Stamp, Julie Christie, John Hurt, Oliver Reed, and so on.

But, by the early 70's, British Cinema was in free-fall, with the once-mighty *Rank* in disarray, and *British Lion* reduced to making only a few films a year.

In 1970, *EMI (Electric & Musical Industries),* which was making a fortune from The Beatles, bought *Associated British*

Pictures, re-named it *EMI Films*, and appointed Bryan Forbes to run it.

Forbes announced he was going to 'revitalize British Cinema' but the *EMI* Board mysteriously starved him of capital. Despite this, he did well with movies like *The Railway Children, The Tales of Beatrix Potter* and *The Go-Between,* and turned his paltry £4m start-up capital into £18m by the time he was pushed out by Nat Cohen, an *EMI* executive and rival.

In 1976, *EMI Films* bought *British Lion*.

British Lion's Barry Spikings and Michael Deeley were put in charge and made several memorable films – such as *'The Man Who Fell To Earth,'* starring David Bowie – but most of the pictures they made were done with Hollywood partners.

And when you have a partner, you have a boss.

Ruth Barton, writing about co-productions in *'Seventies British Cinema,'* [5] observed that:

'The overall effect of these co-productions [...] is a hiatus between their sense of place, character and narrative. Visually, they play on the fetishistic display of glamorous... locations as a kind of vicarious tourism, a phenomenon more usually associated with the James Bond cycle. Another common production trick was to cast unlikely actors in lead and, particularly, secondary roles – one thinks here of the appearance of O J Simpson and Ava Gardner alongside Sophia Loren and Richard Harris in *The Cassandra Crossing*, or Jon Voigt performing with a German accent in *The Odessa File*.'

The 1970's saw British Cinema disintegrate.

---

[5] Edited Robert Shail, Palgrave Macmillan, 2008.

First, *Associated British Pictures* went down, then *The Rank Organisation,* then *British Lion, Ealing Studios, and Tigon.* Then *Hammer Films,* followed by the 'Carry-On' films. Then *Amicus*, which had made *The House That Dripped Blood, Tales From the Crypt,* and *The Land that Time Forgot.*

By 1980, only *EMI Films* was left.

Then disaster struck.

In 1983, Margaret Thatcher's government abolished the Eady Levy, the National Film Finance Corporation *and* the Film Quota.

EMI Films went belly-up.

There was an anguished howl of protest from the film community, led by Sir Richard Attenborough, Sean Connery, Michael Caine, and Norman St John Stevas - Margaret Thatcher's Arts Minister.

When asked by Norman St John Stevas why she wouldn't restore the quota, Thatcher said: "Because that would violate the principles of Free Trade."

But British Cinema wasn't going down without a fight.

During the '80's and '90's, various heroic individuals burst on the scene.

David Puttnam and Sandy Lieberson, of *Goldcrest Films*, made successful movies like: *Chariots Of Fire, The Mission, The Killing Fields, Local Hero,* and *Memphis Belle.*

George Harrison and Denis O'Brien set up *HandMade Films* and made 24 pictures, including: *Withnail & I, The Life of Brian,* and *Time Bandits.*

Lew Grade launched *ITC Entertainment* with *Raise the Titanic, Saturn 3, Legend of the Lone Ranger, Sophie's Choice,*

On Golden Pond, and *The Dark Crystal.* He also financed *The Long Good Friday* but didn't release it.[6]

Sadly, Lew Grade's ITC was sunk by *Raise The Titanic,* an expensive flop about which he said later: "It would have been cheaper to raise the Atlantic!"

The innovative Nik Powell founded *Palace Pictures* by releasing films through video stores. He made *Hardware, Dust Devil, The Company of Wolves,* and many others.

Verity Lambert used TV to fund and promote British movies, and made a success of *Euston Films.*

Jeremy Thomas produced popular art movies like: *Bad Timing, Merry Christmas Mr. Lawrence, The Last Emperor,* and *Naked Lunch.*

David Rose made a massive contribution to British films by founding *Film on Four* in 1981. Under Jeremy Isaacs, the head of Channel Four, Rose financed 136 movies between 1981 and 1990, including: *Dance with a Stranger, My Beautiful Laundrette, Wish You Were Here, High Hopes,* and *Rita, Sue and Bob Too.*

In 1990, the new head of Channel Four, Michael Grade, asked David Aukin to run the film division.

Aukin built on the success of David Rose by commissioning over 100 features including *Shallow Grave* (d. Danny Boyle, 1994,) and *Four Weddings and A Funeral* (d. Mike Newell, 1994).

In 1998, Paul Webster replaced David Aukin and changed *Film4*'s policy from fully-funding British films to investing in American co-productions.

---

[6] It was bought by George Harrison's *HandMade Films,* and released by Paramount.

In 2002, after mounting losses, *Film4* was closed down.

'For two decades, the film subsidiary of Channel 4 was the nearest thing Britain had to a movie studio. Yesterday's demise of Film4 brings a rich, intriguing era to a close and deprives British filmmakers of a significant funding source in what is already an arid financial spell...'

David Gritten

Daily Telegraph - 09 July 2002

Simon Relph, at the state-funded *British Screen*, backed more than 50 movies. His successor, Simon Perry, pioneered new sources of European funding and, between 1992 and 1999, spawned over 60 British features.

Richard Branson put his toe in the water with *The Great Rock 'n' Roll Swindle* (d. Julien Temple), *Nineteen Eighty-Four* (d. Michael Radford), and *Electric Dreams* (d. Steve Barron.)

And movies were made by auteurs on shoestring budgets.

These auteurs included Peter Greenaway, Derek Jarman, Alan Clarke, Alex Cox, and Chris Petit – aided by independent producers like Don Boyd, Clive Parsons and Davina Belling.

But none of these gallant individuals could sustain their careers, let alone revive British Cinema.

Lew Grade abandoned motion pictures in 1982. *Virgin Films* shut down in '86. Sandy Lieberson's *Goldcrest Films* - once heralded as 'the saviour of the British Film Industry' - tip-toed away in '87. *Palace Pictures* expired in '92,[7] and *HandMade* went broke in '94.

The only studio to survive was *PolyGram Filmed Entertainment.*

In 1991, Michael Kuhn became head of *PolyGram* with $200 million in start-up capital. In order to have access to the American market, most of the films he made were U.S. co-productions - but 20 were British.

Kuhn's last film was the Trudie Styler-backed *Lock, Stock and Two Smoking Barrels* (d. Guy Ritchie.)

Under Michael Kuhn, *PolyGram's* track record was better than any Hollywood studio. As a result, he was seen as a threat, and a substantial offer was made to *PolyGram's* parent company, *Phillips Electronics.*

Polygram was purchased, as part of a $10.4 billion deal, by *Seagram's*, the owner of *Universal Studios*, and swiftly broken up. This wasn't personal, it was business. It's called 'getting rid of the competition.'

In 2000, the newly established *UK Film Council* provided finance for three potential studios named *DNA, The Film Consortium* and *Pathé Productions*. A number of films were made but they all failed and, in 2004, the scheme was abandoned.

Throughout the 90's, the BBC had made about one film a year but, in 2000, it upped its game and co-financed five: *Wonder Boys, Wild About Harry, Maybe Baby, Saltwater, Shadow of the Vampire*, and *Billy Elliot.*

---

[7] Nik Powell later resumed making films through his new company *Scala Productions.*

By 2016, its creative director, Christine Langan, was part-funding eight films a year on an annual budget of £12 million.

"The BBC are investing £12 million in eight films a year that are shown on BBC2 – not on BBC1. So, they're thinking of the feature films as a BBC2 audience, which is odd when you want to have commercially successful feature films. But they're only able to contribute a maximum of one and a half million pounds [...] and you can't really make a film for less than two and a half million pounds in this country. So, the BBC will never be able to fully fund a film."

John Goldschmidt

At the time of writing, the BBC's latest film, *Mindhorn,* is a delightful British comedy, which we used to make a lot of, but is now, sadly, a great rarity.

Britain, which invented the movies, and created the world's second biggest film industry, now makes fewer indigenous films than Denmark. Our once magnificent film industry has been almost completely obliterated.

How did this happen?

Chapter Two
SCREEN WEST MIDLANDS

"Some people get the good life
...others get it up the ass."

Once Upon a Time in America

The first UK film organisation we investigated was our local screen agency: *Screen West Midlands.*

Screen West Midlands obtained its funding from the *UK Film Council,* the *National Lottery, the European Union,* and (supposedly) private sources. Their remit was to 'support and nurture emerging local filmmakers,' and to 'create a sustainable UK film industry.'

To get some idea of what they were doing, we watched the films they'd funded, which were mostly digital shorts. A good many were available online but others were hard to find. The films were of wildly different quality and, in terms of content, quite random.

What was the agency's selection process?

We'd already had some contact with *Screen West Midlands,* when we were applicants for funding.

On that occasion, my application had not been successful and the feedback report had been laconic. It was one sentence: *"Would like to work with further."*

I'd never worked with Screen West Midlands before, so this was puzzling. Hoping for clarification - and a bit of nurturing - I asked if I could discuss my script with the person who'd assessed it. My request was refused, because my assessor's identity was 'protected under the Data Protection Act.'

Robin Dutta's feedback was even more frustrating. It stated he hadn't included a budget or a schedule (which he had), and that he'd never directed before, despite his giving them details - and DVDs - of three of his short films. What's more, his screenplay - a bleak, kitchen-sink drama - was described as a comedy!

We'd also had an indirect connection with our local screen agency, which occurred in 2006 when a large sum of public money, labelled *Mediabox,* was launched through Screen West Midlands. The money was earmarked for underprivileged teenagers.

Robin and I, while working as videographers for Birmingham City Council, had made friends with three local charities: *The Youth Inclusion Programme, Soho Youths*, and *KAPS (Keeping Adolescents Protected and Safe.)*

We informed them about *Mediabox.*

As a result, the charities told their kids about it, and took meetings with a person named Lou Llewellyn at SW Midlands who also worked for a group called *The Rural Media Company.*

The next time we saw the people from *KAPS*, we asked them how they'd got on at Screen West Midlands and were told: "Those funds were already ring-fenced for others."

The upshot was that a hefty proportion of the Mediabox funds went to The Rural Media Company.

At the *Birmingham Screen Festival* (where I had a short film in competition), Screen WM came out in force. We tried, in vain, to talk to them. As we were leaving, a cinema manager told us he'd heard one of them say: "I don't know why people keep applying to us. We only fund our friends!"

We investigated the films sponsored by Screen WM and found that the daughter of Sunandan Walia, an ex-panel member, had received funding for two short films. And Sunandan Walia himself had received £29,750 for 'script development.' Also, an ex- Screen West Midlands manager, named Paul Green, had been funded to make a short film called *Mutton*.

We discovered they'd put a six-figure sum into a London-based BBC TV series, called *Hustle,* owned by Elizabeth Murdoch.[8]

For an agency with a remit to 'support and nurture' talent in the West Midlands, this seemed extraordinary.

When we interviewed Nigel Hastilow[9], he said:

"It's a little club. And you do end up with the sense that 'you scratch my back and I'll scratch yours.' It's a very closed unit. Everybody knows everybody. There's not much room for people to break in and gain new ground because it's a closed shop. The temptation for public sector bodies is to look after their own. I was intrigued by the fact that Screen West Midlands was paying £400,000 to help, effectively, Elizabeth Murdoch."

We went to a seminar arranged by Screen West Midlands on 'How to Pitch Your Applications.'

---

[8] Daughter of Rupert Murdoch, CEO of News Corp, Harper Collins, Sky Television, Fox movie studios, Fox TV, and Sky. Elizabeth Murdoch had also been a member of the UK Film Council.

[9] Author and erstwhile Conservative Party candidate for the Halesowen & Rowley Regis constituency.

At the Q&A session, someone in the audience asked: "What do you have to do to get in with Screen West Midlands?"

Someone yelled out: "Join in with them doing lines!"[10]

This provoked much laughter.

Later, we found a *Birmingham Post* article headlined: *"Row Over Board Members."*

It included the following:

"Since the beginning of the agency's life there have been tense and frequently unacknowledged discussions in the sector about the number of times beneficiaries turned out to be the companies of Screen WM board members."[11]

The CEO of Screen West Midlands was Edward J. Turpie, the owner of a TV production company called *Maverick TV*. We wrote to him, asking for an interview, but he didn't get back to us.

The directors of two TV companies (*Hotbed Media* and *Dreamfinder Productions*) were also on the board of Screen WM. Was there a conflict of interest here? We needed to find out.

We wondered if we could use the Freedom of Information Act to get access to *Screen West Midlands'* books.

We approached Gisela Stuart, our local Member of Parliament.

Here's what she wrote:

"I have checked with the Commons and the Library assures me that Screen WM is covered by The Freedom Of Information legislation..."

---

[10] Lines of cocaine.

[11] By Roger Shannon, Professor of Film at Edge Hill University, and the producer of the witty *Festival* (2005), *Beautiful People* (1999), *My Brother Tom* (2001) and *Lawless Heart* (2002).

With help from Gisela Stuart, M.P., our information requests were sent to *Screen West Midlands*.

Six weeks later, we received replies to most of our questions.

But the names of beneficiaries were not disclosed on the grounds that they were "SECTION 43 exemptions."

SECTION 43 exempts information, disclosure of which would be likely to prejudice the commercial interests of any person. It also includes a specific exemption for trade secrets. It protects not only the commercial interests of third parties but also the commercial interests of the public authority that holds the information. In using this exemption, you should bear in mind that the commercial sensitivity (particularly the market sensitivity) of information will usually decrease with time. This exemption is subject to the public interest test.

We wrote back asking Screen West Midlands to let us have the names of the beneficiaries because it was in the public interest for the public to know who was getting public money.

This was the reply:

"With regards to the previous Section 43 exemptions, we consider this an appropriate response."

We wrote to the Information Commissioner. His reply:

'Screen West Midlands does not have a duty to respond to information requests made under FOIA.'

The Commissioner also said that not only was Screen West Midlands exempt from the FOI Act but so were *all* the UK Screen Agencies, and the British Film Institute, The British Film Commission, *and* the UK Film Council.

We were dumbfounded. Where were we? Soviet Russia?

Later, when we talked to Lord Chris Smith,[12] he was equally perplexed.

"I had assumed that any public body with public appointments made by the Secretary of State and largely dependent on public money was, indeed, under the Freedom of Information Act."

Nonetheless, the incomplete information we'd received from the FOI indicated that some Screen West Midlands members may well have been funding their own companies.

The information we gathered is set out below.

MAVERICK TV

+ Dance TV, Hi8us Midlands, Hi8us Edrama, Hi8us Projects Ltd.

(Edward J. Turpie, director.)

E. J. Turpie was a director of SWM from 17/09/01 - 30/06/08

Date	Project	Source	Amount
2002	Crossovers	FOI	£20,000
2002	Ideas Factory	FOI	£17,000
2004	Ideas Factory	FOI	£10,000
2004	Rolling Stock	FOI	£4,967
2005	Hi8us 1stLight	ENHANCE & ADVANCE	£5,000
2005	Lucinda Cattel	ENHANCE & ADVANCE	£3,050
2005	Hi8us (Midlands) Ltd	FOI & PROJECTING STOKE	£10,000
2006	Peter Jones	MOVING UP	£1,000
2006	Dance TV	LOTTERY GRANT	£4,725
2007	Dance Xchange		£50,000
2007	Hi8us Edrama		£50,000

TOTAL: £175,742

---

[12] Ex-Secretary of State for Culture, Media and Sport. Author of 'A Future for British Film' - recommendations to Government re: UK Film Policy.

HOTBED MEDIA

(Johanna Dyer, director)

Johanna Dyer was a director of SWM from 16/01/02 – 30/09/11

Date	Project	Source	Amount
2003	Hotbed Media	FOI	£5,558
2005	Tiffany Ballou	MOVING UP	£1,000
2005	Hotbed Media	Birmingham Post	£17,500
2006	Lucy Mallins	MOVING UP	£1,000
2006	Alex Jones	MOVING UP	£1,000
2006	(Repaid)	Birmingham Post	-£9,231
2007	Hotbed Media	Birmingham Post	£26,700
2008	Hotbed Media	Birmingham Post	£25,000
2009	Love Radio	FOI	£7,000

TOTAL: £75,527

DREAMFINDER PRODUCTIONS

(Natasha Carlish, director.)

N. Carlish was a director of SWM from 13/10/2006 - 07/05/2010.

Date	Project	Source	Amount
2002	Eave	FOI	£1,020
2002	Black Country Western	FOI	£6,670
2004	Ghostlife	FOI	£7,000
2005	Christine James script	FOI	£7,000
2005	West Side Stories 2	FOI	£8,280
2005	Brummiewood	FOI	£18,800
2005	Mr Microscope	RIFE	£7,000
2006	Producer's Forum	RIFE	£23,500
2006	Mr Microscope	RIFE	£905
2006	Advantage Development	Annual Review	£30,000
2006	New Directions film	MAGIC SCREEN	£660
2006	Training Value	Annual Review	£3,500
2006	Carleen Jackson	MOVING UP	£1,000

2008	The Show Must Go On	FOI	£10,000
2008	Soul Boy	Birmingham Post	£368,000
2008	Producer's Forum	Lottery Grant	£20,000
2008	Grand Union	FOI	£19,725

TOTAL: £533,060

As part of our research, we caught a media event at Saint Martin's Church, in Birmingham, where we met Susi O'Neill. O'Neill was involved in a funding agency called *'Advantage West Midlands.'*[13]

As we chatted, she told us she was about to transfer a seven-figure sum to Screen WM but was hesitant about releasing it.

"I get a load of complaints about Screen West Midlands," she said - and asked us for any information we had about them.

Happy to oblige, we sent her an outline of apparent conflicts of interest.

Later, we learned that Screen WM got the seven-figure sum from Advantage West Midlands and that Edward J. Turpie - Screen WM's CEO - was also on the board of Advantage West Midlands.[14]

"If people are prepared to put themselves forward and make a contribution to the industry by taking up a place on the board of a Regional Screen Agency, for example, then part of the deal is that, by doing that, they rule themselves out as possible recipients of the money that that same organisation is distributing...If it's true that you have an organization in receipt

---

[13] *Advantage West Midlands* was one of nine Regional Development Agencies in England, created by the European Commission. Susi O'Neill's title was: 'Screen Image & Sound Cluster Manager.'

[14] E J Turpie is now on the board of *Creative England*, successor of the *UK Film Council*.

of public money that's distributing that public money to members of its own board, there are serious questions to be asked about the proper governance of that organization."

Martin Spence

Assistant General Secretary of BECTU
The media and entertainment union.

In 2009, the TaxPayers' Alliance revealed that Screen West Midlands spent £23,500 on 'entertaining.' We wondered who they were entertaining.

It certainly wasn't emerging, local filmmakers.

*

We were kindly granted an interview with John Woodward, the ex-Chief Executive Officer of the UK Film Council.

QUESTION: Can you comment on what qualified Suzi Norton to be CEO of Screen West Midlands?

WOODWARD: No, but I think Suzi Norton did a good job there, overall. That's my perception.

QUESTION: Her husband recently produced a feature documentary called *The Last Projectionist*. Would it have been permissible for him to be in receipt of public funds via the Screen West Midlands screen agency?[15]

WOODWARD: Phew! Well, there's a question! I think the answer is, almost certainly, 'yes,' because I think it almost would have been illegal to refuse to, at least, consider him for funds because

---

[15] In section 5.5 of the Framework Agreement between the UK Film Council and Screen West Midlands, it states: *"The RSA (Regional Screen Agency) shall inform the UKFC of any instances of conflict of interest..."*

you would be discriminating against him on the grounds that he has a relationship with someone employed in a body that gives out public money. I think what would have happened is that a structure would have been created that removed any conflict of interest so that there couldn't have been any conflict – or, indeed, any *perception* of any conflict in the decision making. That's certainly what one would have wanted.

QUESTION: Isn't that just a loophole?

WOODWARD: That depends. I've no idea what the circumstances were. But one would assume that, in those situations, there is a very clear separation, and a degree of governance around that, because whenever you get anywhere even close to those situations, it's common sense that a decision like that is going to be scrutinized very, very heavily. You're not going to be able to get away with that without people going: "Well, how did that happen?" So, more often than not, people are actually *twice* as careful, rather than less careful, about how they handle themselves.

QUESTION: Would you have regarded it as permissible for members of the board of Screen West Midlands to have funded their own companies?

WOODWARD: Look, I don't know what you're referring to, but I think you need to be quite careful in what you're saying. The board of Screen West Midlands funded its own companies?

QUESTION: Yes. You had Natasha Carlish on the board of Screen West Midlands who funded 'Dreamfinder Productions' – her company – and you had Jonnie Turpie, on the board – as well as a former CEO of Screen West Midlands – who...

WOODWARD: I think what you would find - if you dig into that - is there were processes... Does Screen West Midlands still exist?

QUESTION: No. They're one of the few that have closed now.

WOODWARD: Okay. I think what you would find, if you dig in, is that there were careful procedures to make sure that those conflicts of interest were addressed, and separated out. So, I can't comment on that kind of accusation.

QUESTION: Well, it's an observation more than an accusation. It's not an accusation because it's not illegal. And it's about perception. If the perception is 'these funds are not for us,' then, naturally, there will be a decrease in applications for Lottery funding – which is what we saw.[16]

WOODWARD: With respect, it doesn't sound as if you're coming at this from a particularly objective point of view. You sound rather like you're coming at this as someone who is quite disappointed not to have received funding themselves.

QUESTION: Not at all.

WOODWARD: (Smiling.) It just comes across that way.

QUESTION: It's just that there is criticism...

WOODWARD: But there's always criticism of public bodies in that respect... When you're the holder of public money, there's never enough money to give to everyone... And the people who get it are happy, and...the people who don't are embittered...But the problem for the people in positions of power, on the other side of the desk - who are trying to make sure the money is spent

---

[16] In the UK Film Council's final year, there was a 32% decrease in applications for Lottery funding.

wisely - is that they can't give everyone money. So, inevitably, you end up with an awful lot of people who are disappointed. Now, whether the right decisions or the wrong decisions are made, is a matter for endless debate."

We interviewed Scott Johnston, an emerging local filmmaker who made a short called *Kraft*, starring Tom Bell, which was funded by Screen West Midlands.

"What was it like dealing with them?" we asked.

"They have no knowledge or understanding of how to work with filmmakers. All they care about is organising trips to Cannes, strutting around like film moguls, and playing one-upmanship games with other cultural bureaucrats like themselves."

Scott was especially peeved by Screen West Midlands board members who awarded themselves producer credits merely for being in the room when a cheque was signed.

We also interviewed emerging local filmmaker Mark Jeavons.

"Independent filmmakers who are in the West Midlands can't get their foot in the door. They cannot be seen, or heard, or nurtured. And when it's yourself, and it's your own project, which you're producing and directing, and you're not supported, it's like you against the world. And filmmaking is such a difficult thing. If you're going to do a feature film, you need as much support as possible, and that's what the regional screen agencies should have been there to do.

I think, in America, it's different. If you look at Kevin Smith, or Robert Rodriguez, they started off making very small films. And they were supported – and celebrated – in the U.S. Whereas, in the UK, it's looked down upon if you're an independent filmmaker. It's almost like a dirty word."

Mark Jeavons.

Was Screen West Midlands typical of every regional screen agency, or was it an exception?

We would have to find out.

Chapter Three
REGIONAL SCREEN AGENCIES

"The Regional Screen Agencies, legally and financially, were responsible to the UK Film Council and the Partnership Team within the UK Film Council. But there were all kinds of complicated discussions around legitimacy because the screen agencies were obviously responsible to the UK Film Council for the proportion of their money that came from the UK Film Council, but they were not responsible to the Film Council for the money they got from elsewhere, and for the commercial funds that they raised. They were deliberately constituted by the UK Film Council as independent companies. So, it wasn't like they were the regional branches of the UK Film Council - each one was an independent company - but they got their core funding and their core remit from the Film Council. They had started with a very simple, tight remit about supporting talent and supporting audience development in the regions, but this changed."

John Newbigin
Chairman of Creative England

Our next interview was with an emerging multi-media artist named Lea Walton.

We asked him what he thought of the British film industry.

"The British Film industry is a myth – and anyone who believes the Screen Agencies support new talent is stupid [...] There are many highly paid people in the UK, whose only job is to keep their job."

We needed a rejoinder to Lea Walton's opinions, so we contacted the Regional Screen Agencies. These were:

Screen East (East of England),

EM Media (East Midlands),

Film London (Greater London),

Northern Film & Media (North East England),

Vision & Media (North West England),

Screen South (South East England),

South West Screen (South West England),

Screen West Midlands (West Midlands),

Screen Yorkshire (Yorkshire and the Humber).

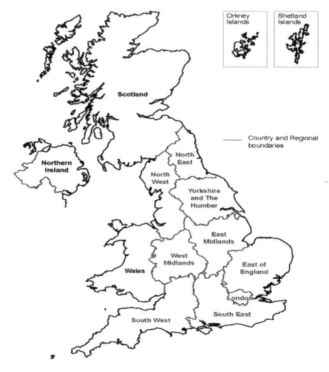

Contains Ordnance Survey data © Crown copyright and database right 2013

These regions correspond with the EU Administration Zones created in 1994 to prepare for the UK's absorption into the United States of Europe.

Every screen agency received money from the EU.

As I write this, 'Article 50' has been triggered, and the government is negotiating an exit from the European Union. If this happens, these administrative zones - together with their unelected assemblies – will, hopefully, be scrapped.

In any event, all the Regional Screen Agencies refused to speak to us. Why? Were they afraid of criticism? Or were they up to no good?

In at least one case, they *were* up to no good.

In 2010, *Screen East* went bankrupt after its finance director, Melvin Welton, was jailed for embezzlement.

'Screen East, the regional screen agency for the east of England, is no longer operating following insolvency, and the arrest of its finance manager, Melvin Welton, on suspicion of theft, it has been confirmed today.

Laurie Hayward, chief executive of Screen East told Screen that: "The directors of Screen East have concluded that the company is insolvent and can't meet its debts as they fall due. The directors have taken advice and are appointing an insolvency practitioner to take the company into administration.'

SCREEN DAILY 10 September, 2010

We asked John Woodward, the ex-CEO of the UK Film Council, what qualifications were needed to become the director of a regional screen agency.

WOODWARD: (Smiles.) These are very, very strange questions. What qualifications? Well, management ability, strategic skills - one would hope - leadership in a broad sense - I would put those in the key block - and I think if you're running a screen agency, well, what you then have, within your team, is a bunch of other, rather more specific, skills that are tailored to the activity areas.

QUESTION: And what about film experience?

WOODWARD: Well, I think film and audio-visual production experience, finance experience, distribution experience – yes – all of that is helpful.

QUESTION: What does a CEO of a screen agency do to merit a six-figure salary? Or should the Ministry have capped this?

WOODWARD: Well, I think the thing about labour is that it's about supply and demand and what you can command in the market place for your particular skills. We live in a world where those are negotiations that are freely held between employers and employees. In the public sector, there's a degree of regulation around that in terms of what governments – or local governments – think is acceptable. But the reality is that individuals will always seek to maximize their own salary in any negotiation..."

When we put this question to the director, Sir Alan Parker - an ex-head of the UK Film Council - he said:

"We gave the regions autonomy."

When we asked Lord Smith, he said:

"Our review didn't look at personnel and, actually, we shouldn't have because none of us were in a position to make judgements about who was making a real contribution and who wasn't."

We still don't know what qualified people to be appointed to screen agencies, or how their salaries were arrived at. All we know is that having no film experience was not a problem.

"In terms of the constant group that were there (at Screen West Midlands) [...] there seemed to be a lack of film people."

Professor Roger Shannon.

As our research progressed, it became increasingly evident that the Regional Screen Agencies were failing to meet their remit.

With one exception: *East Midlands Media.*

Unhappily, they turned down every request we made to speak with them. They told us they didn't like 'the slant of the documentary.' What slant was that? All we were doing was seeking the truth!

This was a shame because we venerated what EM Media was doing. It was the only agency actually trying to build a sustainable UK film industry.

During the 10 years of its existence, EM Media backed 42 British feature films, and set up a distribution company to get their films into cinemas.

Led by Ken Hay, Debbie Williams and Lisa Opie, EM Media gave support to *Warp Films*, the Sheffield-based production company that launched Shane Meadows (*This is England*, 2006), Chris Morris (*The Four Lions*, 2010), Justin Kurzel, (*Snowtown*, 2011), and Richard Ayoade (*Submarine*, 2010, and *The Double*, 2013).

Unlike the other screen agencies, EM Media had film people on its board, including one of our best movie directors, Stephen Frears, a native of Leicester.

Below are some of the films they made - many excellent, all British.

Anita & Me (2002)

Once Upon a Time in the Midlands (2002)

One for the Road (2003)

Dead Man's Shoes (2004)

A Cock and Bull Story (2005)

This Is England (2006)

Over the Hill (2007)

The Imaginary Girl (2007)

When Did You Last See Your Father? (2007)

Control (2007)

Daddy's Girl (2007)

Rebecca (2007)

The Visitor (2007)

Bronson (2008)

Mum & Dad (2008)

Better Things (2008)

Donkey Punch (2008)

Crying with Laughter (2009)

Tender (2009)

Unmade Beds (2009)

No Lady (2010)

A Shining Light (2010)

God of Animals (2010)

Skeletons (2010)

This Side of the Afterlife (2010)

Tyrannosaur (2011)

Entity (2012)

The Great Hip Hop Hoax (2013)

When future historians study the culture of our time, they will undoubtedly study EM Media's films.

The regional screen agencies were established in 2000, by the UK Film Council, employing the corporatist model - also known as PPP (Public Private Partnership). This model merges big Business with Government.

Before the advent of Corporatism – brought in by Margaret Thatcher in 1980, which privatized the railways and monetized the National Health Service - Government acted as a referee between the Public and Business - with the public interest often prevailing over the business interest.

Under the corporatist model, Government and Big Business combine *against* the interests of the public.

Corporatist ideology can be summed up in the phrase: "What's good for General Motors is good for America." A little reflection reveals this dictum to be false. What the public wants is choice and low prices; what General Motors wants is a monopoly (no choice) and high profits. What's good for General Motors is actually *bad* for America.

The British Film Commission is an example of corporatism. From its plush offices in Beverly Hills, it offers Hollywood players financial incentives to make their movies in Britain.

The Film Commission is a division of *Film London*, a private limited company funded by the taxpayer and the National Lottery. *Film London* doesn't make profits because it's a registered charity. The profits go to the owners of our production houses (Pinewood, Shepperton, Beaconsfield etc.), and to other smaller businesses such as equipment rental houses, post-production firms, and catering companies.

1) Each year, the government donates millions of pounds to a charity.

2) The charity uses the cash to induce US companies to make films in the UK.

3) As a result, Hollywood movies like *Batman*, *Star Wars*, *James Bond* and *Harry Potter,* are made in Britain. Each big-budget production may well spend over $100 million on rents, products, and services.

4) This benefits the economy.

Clearly, this is good for business, but is it good for the public? Some say 'yes, it is.' And they say the British don't like British films. They'd rather watch American films.

Before the corporatist UK Film Council, we had the quasi-socialist Film Commissions and *British Screen* - which supported movies like *The Mystery of Edwin Drood* (1993) and *Brassed Off* (1996.) The people who steered *British Screen* were experienced film producers, such as Simon Relph.[17]

From 1986 to 1991, Relph backed over 50 British films, including *Room With A View, Empire State,* and *A World Apart.*

From 1992 to 1999, British Screen was run by Simon Perry, who championed over 60 British features, including: *Orlando* (d. Sally Potter), *Sister My Sister* (d. Nancy Meckler), *Richard III* (d. Richard Loncraine), *Victory* (d. Mark Peploe), *Photographing Fairies* (d. Nick Willing), *Hilary and Jackie* (d. Anand Tucker), *Among Giants* (d. Sam Miller), *The Clandestine Marriage* (d. Chris Miles), *Bread & Roses* (d. Ken Loach), and *Bend It Like Beckham* (d. Gurinder Chadha.)

---

[17] Relph produced *Reds* (1981), *The Return of the Soldier* (1982), *The Ploughman's Lunch* (1983), *Wetherby* (1985), *Comrades* (1986), *Enchanted April* (1992), *The Secret Rapture* (1993), *Blue Juice* (1995), *Slab Boys* (1997), *The Land Girls* (1998), *Hideous Kinky* (1998).

The UK Film Council and Regional Screen Agencies, which replaced British Screen and the Film Commissions, weren't staffed by people experienced in film.

"I still have no idea why a job of such delicacy should go to someone who has no experience. It's beyond me. And I'm still staggered...The UK Film Council developed the Regional Screen Agencies and folded up the Film Commissions. It was a sad time, and also a destructive time, because over the preceding 10 years, the Film Commissions were going from strength to strength and doing a fantastic job in the regions. What we saw was the complete demolition of that network."

Liz Rymer
Former CEO of the Yorkshire Film Commission

"It did feel as though anyone who knew anything in the film industry was being sent out to plant rice in the paddy fields."

John Gore
Warwick Arts Centre

We asked John Woodward, ex-CEO of the UK Film Council, why the Film Commissions were replaced by the Regional Screen Agencies.

WOODWARD: The provision of support outside of London, which is where 95% of the commercial film industry exists [...] provision for local filmmakers, for local exhibition, for training activity, for different cultural initiatives around film, was very patchy and unserved. The only coherent network there was - in 2000 - was a film commission network that was focused on providing advice and support for inward investment: i.e. for feature filmmakers and TV productions, to a certain extent, who were shopping around to try and work out where they could shoot a film. There was no regional strategy that worked properly. There was provision in some areas. There were initiatives that were being supported on a piece-meal basis – but there wasn't any kind of coherent approach. And the level of investment - when we added it up - was tiny. So, what the UK Film Council did was to make a coherent strategy, which was to set up an agency in the different English regions; to have a separate set of relationships with the screen agencies in Scotland, Wales, and Northern Ireland, and to pump money into them over a period of years, on the grounds that not everyone wanted to live and work in London; and there were talents and voices working outside of London that weren't getting heard.

QUESTION: Who was responsible for the Regional Screen Agencies? Was there some sort of governance, or were they independent?

WOODWARD: They were basically independent. That was always the thinking behind them; because, again, it was about us wanting to get away from the sense that everything had to be controlled from London. So, we set them up at the Film Council but the ambition was, literally, to set them up as legal entities; to appoint some board members who came from the regions; to agree a funding agreement that delivered some national priorities, in terms of activities and outputs, and then, broadly, to go 'good luck.' What we didn't want to do was try to control it from London – control it from the centre. The philosophy was that the people who understand the region best are the people who live and work in that region, so you leave them alone to get on with it."

In March 2011, after the government abolished the UK Film Council, funding for the Regional Screen Agencies was reduced.

But one agency was defunded entirely - *EM Media* - the only successful one.

Why would anyone do that?

"The closing of the East Midlands regional film board was an absolute disgrace! People should be taken out and shot!"

Stephen Frears

Chapter Four
THE UK FILM COUNCIL

"There was not sufficient attention given to the cultural
dimension of the UK Film Council."

John Newbigin
Chairman, Creative England

In March 2011, the UK Film Council was abolished amid cries of protest from British film bureaucrats and Hollywood celebrities such as Clint Eastwood and Steven Spielberg.

But every young filmmaker we interviewed was glad to see it go.

"The UK Film Council was an incestuous facility for a handful of privileged filmmakers."

Nicholas David Lean

"Frankly, trying to get help from the film agencies was more trouble than it was worth."

Jon Rosling

"We did this 35mm pilot (*Darkside of the Earth*), which cost me personally about £38,000 to make. It was shot in a studio in London with this huge set. It had Benedict Cumberbatch in it... What more could I possibly have done?"

Neil Oseman[18]

Some even believed the UK Film Council's purpose was to protect Hollywood's monopoly. Astonishingly, there *is* evidence to support this.

---

[18] Dubbed in media stories as: 'The Spielberg of Hereford.'

In 2004, the CEO of Hollywood's international distribution company (*United International Pictures*) became chairman of the UK Film Council.

'Tidings of great joy from the UK Film Council, which announced over Christmas that 'British films' – including Troy, Alexander, and Harry Potter and the Prisoner of Azkaban – had a record share of US box-office takings in 2004. This follows another triumphant announcement a month earlier when the council boasted that two of the top five films in British cinemas last year had been 'British' – Harry Potter and Troy.

In truth, of course, these films are about as British as Dick van Dyke in Mary Poppins. All their revenues go to Time Warner, an American corporation. As the independent British producer, Jonathan Gems pointed out [...] "we need to place limits on the US distribution cartel, which currently controls 92% of the British market." The cartel in question is United International Pictures, the biggest distribution company in the world, jointly run by the American studios... British and European filmmakers have long argued that UIP uses its monopoly powers to keep local product out of cinemas for the benefit of its owners in California.

But it seems unlikely that the UK Film Council will be throwing its weight behind this campaign. The council's newly appointed chairman, Stewart Till, also happens to be the chairman and chief executive of, er, UIP. Who better to bang the drum and blow the trumpet on behalf of British films than the boss of a company wholly owned by the Hollywood studios!'

Private Eye – 07/01/05

Another sign that the Film Council wasn't a fan of British Cinema was that only a minor portion of its budget went on British films.

"It was good to have one body representing the film industry as a go-between with the government, and (The UK Film Council) did lots of interesting things. But...only 35% of its annual budget was spent on development and production."

John Goldschmidt

When the UK Film Council's closure was announced, some of the loudest protests came from Hollywood. Why would they care about British subsidies being cut? Well, they didn't. The subsidies they cared about were the UK subsidies going to Hollywood.

UK Film Council Senior Staff Remuneration (excluding expenses)

	2009	2010	Bonus
J. Woodward	£210,000	£205,000	£35k-£40k
Colin Brown	£140,000	£145,000	£30k-£35k
P. Buckingham	£135,000	£140,000	£5k-£10k
T. Seghatchian	£165,000	£170,000	
Sally Caplan	£165,000	£170,000	
Will Evans	£155,000	£160,000	
Lenny Crooks	£115,000	£120,000	
Alan Bushell	£110,000	£115,000	
Tim Cagney	£85,000	£90,000	
Oliver Rawlins	£65,000	£70,000	

In addition to the above, large sums were paid into pension schemes and, when the UKFC closed down, scores of employees received lump sums. The cost of these 'exit packages' to the taxpayer totalled £1,484,369.30.

The UK Film Council's greatest failure was in not addressing British films' lack of access to British screens. There is such a strong desire to make films in this country that raising money would be easy if investors could get their money back. But they can't get their money back if British films have no access to a paying public.

After the UK Film Council was shut down, a statement was issued saying that, prior to its abolition, the Council had been thinking about an 'Innovation Fund' *"to provide support for getting films to audiences. But abolition of the organisation meant this fund never became operational."*

Aw! Wot a shame! If only those nasty people in the government hadn't shut down the Film Council, they would have helped British films! They were just about to do it. They were on the verge of doing it. They were poised to do it. But the nasty government shut them down!

The Film Council *always* knew that a sustainable British Film Industry can't exist without screens. That's why, when they were subsidized the digitizing of UK cinemas, they said it was to 'create more screens for British films.'

The UK Film Council gave most of its money to American movie corporations. The rest went on salaries and expenses for its staff, funding for short films no one saw, futile film education initiatives, and public relations exercises.

They did not provide one single screen for British films.

'Congratulations to Tanya Seghatchian who, according to the Guardian, "is now officially the most powerful woman in the British film industry," following her appointment as head of the UK Film Council's new 'unified field fund' with a budget of £15m a year.

Seghatchian was formerly in charge of UKFC's development fund, which made several interesting grants during her stewardship.

In November 2008, there was an award of £70,000 to Apocalypso, which happens to be Tanya's own production company and, last June, £100,000 was given to Heyday Films, her previous employer. Heyday is the co-producer of the Harry Potter films, in which Tanya was closely involved. Quite why it needs a six-figure handout to finance its feature-film development is something of a mystery. The UKFC assures us that its directors "declare any direct interest in award applications" and exclude themselves from "the discussion and decision process" if they have a commercial relationship with recipients of the council's largesse. So that's all right then. But keeping track of all these relationships must be an exhausting job. A list of 'related-party transactions' in the latest accounts reveals that in 2008-09 the UKFC dished out £30m of grants to organisations in which one or more of the directors had a direct interest.'

Private Eye 05/03/10

After the UK Film Council was abolished it was replaced by *Creative England*.

Will Creative England support and nurture the next generation of filmmakers? Will it protect British Cinema from the Hollywood cartel? Will it provide screens for British films? Will it launch British movie studios? Will it create a sustainable UK film industry?

With the best will in the world, Creative England can't do any of those things. It doesn't have the funding or the government support.

So, where will the next Michael Powell, Carol Reed, Jack Cardiff, Richard Attenborough, Lindsay Anderson, David Puttnam, Ken Russell, Mike Hodges, Ken Loach, and Stephen Frears come from?

In 2012, Lord Chris Smith said that, 'in five years,' we could expect to see a 'real impact' and 'change going forward.'

It's now 2017, and the only impacts have been negative – and the only change going forward has been change going backwards.

Chapter Five
THE VIRTUAL PRINT FEE.

"It's a sad time for alternative cinema."

David Lynch

We attended a British Film Institute symposium at a packed-to-the-rafters Midland's Art Centre. The BFI - on a tour of the country - were interested in the 'views and opinions' of the filmmakers in our region.

Many were more than eager to give their views and opinions – especially about the Virtual Print Fee.

The Virtual Print Fee (VPF) is a way to get film distributors to pay for the installation of digital projectors in cinemas. A distributor must pay this fee to every cinema that shows his film.

Hollywood saves money on the VPF from bulk deals with the exhibitors. For them, the VPF is cheaper than duplicating and delivering optical prints. But indie distributors have to pay the same rate as the Hollywood majors.

For example, if an independent distributor is able to negotiate a release of his film in 50 cinemas in the UK, he will, generally, make ten celluloid prints, at a cost of £700 per print, and rotate them around the cinemas. His cost is £7,000.

But if he must pay a £430 Virtual Print Fee to 50 cinemas, his cost is £21,500. And that's only for the first week. If he wants to run his film for a second week, there's a VPF charge of £300 per screen. He must pay another £15,000. Thus, for a two-week run at 50 cinemas, the indie distributer pays a VPF of £36,500 –

compared to just £7,000 for optical prints, which he can store and use many times.

The VPF came down like a hammer on British films.

When asked about the horrors of the VPF, Tim Cagney, the deputy chief executive of the British Film Institute,[19] said:

"I'm not sure the Virtual Print Fee is something a public agency can lead on."

At the end of the event, while the BFI public relations circus was packing up its slides and glossy brochures, someone tugged my arm.

It was a BFI staffer.

"You're on the money with your comments on the virtual print fees," she whispered, "but we're salaried staff, so we can't say anything."

Later, we wrote to the BFI's Tim Cagney to ask for an interview, but he deleted the email without reading it.

The digital projectors and Virtual Print Fee were instigated by the Hollywood studios, and implemented by a tech company called *Arts Alliance Media*, which John Woodward – the ex-CEO of the UK Film Council – was later to run.

WOODWARD: The Virtual Print Fee is a mechanism developed by the cinemas in conjunction with the main distributors, led by the Hollywood Studios. Put very simply, it's a subsidy mechanism whereby the money that will be saved in the long-term by film distributors – because they don't have to make cinema prints of films. That they will be able to use digital files, in one form or

---

[19] And an ex-managing director of the UK Film Council.

another. A proportion of the costs that would have been spent by making celluloid prints are directed back to cinemas to help them pay the very significant costs associated with making the changeover from 35 millimetre to digital. Essentially, it's a massive subsidy to the exhibition sector all around the world.

The mission was cultural in the sense that it was focused at audiences. The idea was, in very broad terms, to say to cinemas: "You want digital equipment. That equipment is very expensive. Our mission at the Film Council is to provide more choice for audiences - and what we know is that...the cost of 35 millimetre prints coming in at five, six, seven hundred pounds a copy – coupled with the sheer difficulty of taking these films on and off projectors for the odd showing here or there for a small niche film - makes it very difficult for the cinemas to run programming strategies that advantage smaller, independent films." So, what we were doing was basically saying that we would subsidize the cinemas to help them get this equipment in, which made them much more flexible as operators and, in exchange for that, we wanted them to play a broader range of films.

And the idea was to look for the optimum number of screens - so it wasn't about trying to pick winners, and saying these are necessarily arthouse cinemas, as opposed to multiplexes. We wanted the cinemas to step forward and say: "We share that vision. We will play more independent films for the period of the deal. And, in exchange for that, we'll get the subsidy." And that's broadly what happened and, somewhere, you can find the statistic that will show you the increase in the number of independent film titles that were put into British cinemas after the digital screen network went in. There's a substantial increase – and that deal was in place for a period of six years, I think it was.

QUESTION: The cinema chains we're talking to are saying they can't play independent films because the independent distributors can't afford the fee.

WOODWARD: Well, no, I think independent distributors are paying VPF's. And independent distributors *like* VPF's because, whichever way you cut it, the cost of supplying a film is going to be less than the cost of making a celluloid print...

When you stand back and take a look at the long view, the VPF is an interim arrangement. VPFs will go at some point in the future because they're all limited. Different deals have different time-frames. But the distributors are not going to continue paying VPFs. There will come a point when the distribution sector will feel it's got enough projectors in cinemas...

The other thing to bear in mind is that, as ever with technology – whether it's flat-screen televisions or professional spec digital film projectors – the cost of that technology is coming down. So, the other thing you're going to see, in three or four years' time, is slightly lower spec projectors on the market at radically-reduced prices.

There will come a time, I believe, when the price point is going to get to a level where the ability to project professional standard images will be at a much lower cost than it is today. I think that's inevitable...

QUESTION: The criticism is that the VPF figure is about £430 to show a film. Now, if MGM has a Bond film showing in 5 screens, that £430 per show isn't much to them but it's a huge amount to an independent distributor.

WOODWARD: But it's still cheaper than a celluloid print.

QUESTION: But a celluloid print can be projected many times. And, if independents incur a fee every time they show a film...

WOODWARD: I don't think they have to pay a fee every time they play it but, inevitably, there's a question for anyone in the business of distributing films about whether or not it's economical to put that film into cinemas. And that's a commercial consideration. And the only solution to that is to provide some form of subsidy, which I have no objection to at all. But if you want to provide some form of subsidy, that's an issue for the government, or the British Film Institute, to say: 'We want to do that.'

Then you would have to ask the question: 'Why do you want to do that?' Why are you giving public money to profit-making distribution companies, or profit-making cinemas or, indeed, charity-based cinemas.

And the only answer to that could be cultural – not economic.

You would subsidize because you think these films need to be supported in the market-place because they don't pay their way commercially.

I think you're attacking the wrong target by attacking VPFs because they are, by definition, a commercial arrangement made between commercial companies, and if there are filmmakers, film distributors, or film exhibitors who feel there's something wrong with that, then their recourse, I think, shouldn't be to complain about commercial arrangements that have been made between private sector companies.

The only recourse is to knock on the door of the government and say: "I make films that, with the best will in the world, can't pay their own way in the market-place and, therefore, I'd like public money to support me. And I think that's reasonable and right. But that's much more complicated, and that's why governments have always had organizations like the Film

Council, or the British Film Institute, to make those kinds of interventions.

With the Film Council, the intervention that was made was to put a bunch of subsidized digital projectors into a broadly geographically spread pattern across the UK, with a commitment from the cinemas that, in exchange for those subsidized projectors, they would book films that they probably otherwise wouldn't have booked.

QUESTION: Couldn't the UK Film Council have been stricter in making sure that those projectors went to the small screens, rather than the large auditoriums?

WOODWARD: No, I don't think that's right...

What we asked for was the maximum commitment for the cinemas to play independent films. And there was a definition of the kind of film we wanted the cinemas to play. And the people who said: 'We will play most of those films' got the projectors. Inevitably, that meant a lot of arthouse cinemas got the projectors because they put their hands up and said: 'That's *all* we play." So, they were very easy – tick the box – they got projectors.

But what also happened is a lot of the cinema-chains got them because, if you're running a large cinema chain and you think there's an audience there for those films, they made a commercial judgement. But they also made a commercial judgement about the type of films they would be able to show and the type of audiences they would get.

I think what the Film Council decided it *didn't* want to do was pick that relatively small number of subsidized arthouse cinemas - who one might loosely call 'the Usual Suspects,' - and say: 'We're just going to give it all to you and we're not going to give anyone else the opportunity. Not least because it probably would have been illegal because I think – under public tender processes - you have to have a process that's open and transparent. And if I'm running a large cinema chain and I took the view that I *did* want to show independent films, why shouldn't I be in exactly the same position to get a projector as a guy who runs an arthouse cinema? We're talking about public money. They all pay taxes."

What infuriated British distributors was the UK Film Council's promise that digital projectors would provide a wider audience for British films.

"We were told: 'multiplexes with 20 screens' - and we're going to get this diversity of films across 20 screens. But we didn't get that. We got 15 screens with *Harry Potter* on, and 5 screens with *Sex in the City 2* on. . ."

Jon Rosling

As I write this, Cineworld, Birmingham Broad Street (which received VPF subsidies), is showing the following - all American - movies:

Batman V Superman

Jungle Book 3D

The Hunstman: Winter's War 3D

Eddie the Eagle

Zootropolis

Midnight Special

We talked to several independent distributors in London. One of them was Alex Hamilton of eOne Films.

"It was a great idea. Put digital projectors into mainstream cinemas to help independent films. The problem was they picked the biggest screens. And the exhibitors always show their biggest Hollywood movies on their biggest screens, so it didn't help independent cinema at all."

For some, the Virtual Print Fee was the last straw and they quit the business. A leading independent distributor, based in Soho, told us they now use 'VPF' as a swear word.

Chapter Six
WHAT IS A BRITISH FILM?

"I got an email from a German woman who'd produced a film. She told me it had been written by a Swiss guy, shot in Germany, directed by a Danish guy, financed in Sweden and France and - in order to be classified as a British film and qualify for a grant - did two weeks' post-production in London."

Jonathan Gems

What is a British film? We'd become quite confused about it. So many American films were being called British that we were losing our grasp of what the word 'British' meant.

Many of the people we interviewed were also confused.

And, why did we need a 'cultural test' to determine whether or not a film was British?

No other country does that.

If *Gravity*[20] had been made in Hungary, would the Hungarians say it was a Hungarian film? Of course not. But *Gravity*, which was made in the UK, is classified as a British film. Why? Because it passed the cultural test.

If your production spends sufficient money in Britain, you will pass the cultural test - and qualify for grants and tax credits.

The cultural test is an ingenious way of bribing foreign film companies to make, or part-make, films in the UK.

---

[20] Dir: Alfondo Cuaron, starring Sandra Bullock (Warner Bros) 2009.

The cultural test is not about culture, it's about money.

War is Peace. Freedom is Slavery. Culture is Money.

George Orwell would have loved it.

'Look closely at posters for Jim Jarmusch's new film Broken Flowers - starring Bill Murray, with Sharon Stone and Jessica Lange – and you'll notice a UK Film Council logo.

Yup, the Film Council's dream of giving British lottery money directly to an all-American feature film has come true.

The seed was planted a few years ago when the council's chairman was Alan Parker, who set out to have as many American movies as possible reclassified as British so that his beloved Hollywood studios could benefit from the tax advantages of 'UK film' status. And now it has been brought to fruition by Parker's successor, Stewart Till.

No surprise there as Till is also chairman and chief executive of UIP, the biggest film distributor in the world – which is owned by the Hollywood studios.'

Private Eye 25/11/05

The real definition of a British film is: a motion picture financed and released by a British movie studio.

Now we have a problem.

How many movie studios do we have?

None.

Our last movie studio was Polygram Filmed Entertainment, which closed in 1998 – almost 20 years ago.

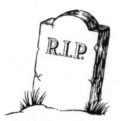

Last studio died 1998

Not only are many confused about what defines a British film, many are also confused about what defines a movie studio.

Our media wants us to think that Pinewood, Shepperton and Elstree are movie studios. They're not.

They're sound-stages.

Warner Bros is a movie studio. It finances and releases films. Paramount is a movie studio. Universal is a film studio. Disney is a film studio. Sony is a film studio. They finance and release films.

Pathé and Gaumont are French film studios. They finance and release French films.

EMI Films, British Lion, Associated British Pictures, and The Rank Organisation were British movie studios, which financed and released British films. But they've gone now.

The movie studio is the hub of the movie business. Its executives decide what scripts to commission, what films to make, who to direct, who to star, which films to release, and how to market them.

The movie studio initiates and controls funding, filmmaking, and distribution. Every decision, although delegated to producers, directors, and others, is ultimately controlled by the executives of the movie studio.

You can't have a film industry without film studios.

Sometimes, a foreign studio will buy a British film that's been made on spec, or made for TV - such as *Priest,*[21] or *Slumdog Millionaire.*[22]

They do this because they can pick up the film cheap and make a profit putting it out. This is known as a 'pick-up.'

But you can't create an industry based on pick-ups because the lion's share of the income goes to the studio that releases the pick-up – not the company that made the film.

The reason there's no British Cinema is there are no British movie studios.

So, why is the media always telling us we have a 'successful British Film industry.' Because, in a sense, we do. Only, it's not British. It's American.

The British Film Commission, the BFI, BAFTA, and, when it existed, the UK Film Council, all had – and have – the same purpose: to procure inward investment.

Inward investment is a term meaning foreign money - most of it coming from Hollywood.

When we asked John Woodward about this, his response was - from his perspective - perfectly reasonable.

WOODWARD: "I think the main purpose of public money should be to secure interesting work that, in creative terms, is something that is not going to be delivered by the market. Because, if it can be delivered by the market, you should leave it to the market to deliver it.

What I think is wrong with your take is that you seem to have an objection to what the commercial sector - and the free market

---

[21] Dir: Antonia Bird (BBC) 1994.
[22] Dir: Danny Boyle (Channel Four) 2008.

- does in terms of filmmaking. And I think you're wrong-headed in that approach.

I think the film industry is the film industry. It's commercial and it makes decisions that are in its own best commercial interests.

And, in the end, that's all funnelled down to what audiences want...

You can make arguments – good arguments – for why public money should be used to support the economic development of the industry, but that needs to be done very carefully – and not in a boastful manner.

In the end, the most important thing is [...] to try and identify the talent and give them the time and resources they need to tell stories that the market - left to its own devices – is not going to deliver.

Because, quite often, the stuff that is really interesting in the mainstream of tomorrow, is the stuff that's really innovative, and new, and difficult, and challenging to do today.

The market tends to follow success that's gone before.

I think the most important thing that public money can do is take risks on voices that haven't been heard.

Now, the problem with voices that haven't been heard is that, overwhelmingly, most of those voices don't have very much to say.

And that's where it all gets tricky because what you have to do is find out who are the people who've really got something interesting to say that's going to resonate – and who are the people who, frankly, are not very good.

And that is why, to an extent, running a public-sector funder of film or television is - as in any other creative industry - always very difficult because it's impossible to take out subjective taste [...] And, taking risks on talent that is new and untried, fundamentally, is the most productive thing for the public sector to do.

There are also very good reasons why public money is spent supporting the inward investment of [...] big-budget Hollywood films. They are very real and substantial contributors to the British economy, and they support our own talent and you can't separate them out from the indigenous talent base."

By touting for inward investment, the British Film Commission is an agent of cultural treachery.

When the British Academy of Film and Television Arts gives awards to American films, it's sleeping with the enemy.

When the government gives our money to foreign film studios, it's committing cultural treason. If it wants to invest in films, let them be British films.

In 2008, only 9 British films were released in the UK, but the BFI and the UK Film Council claim 45 British films were released.

Which figure is correct?

First, let's use common sense. If 45 new British films came out in 2008, that's almost one a week. That's a lot. You have to go back as far as 1962 to find a year that released that many British films.

Forty-five new British movies would have made a big impact. Who were the new British movie stars these movies launched? Who are all the new writers and directors?

Well, there was no major impact - no explosion of new talent.

So, what *were* these British films?

44 Inch Chest	CANADA
Awaydays	**UK** Red Union
The Boat That Rocked	U.S. Universal
Boogie Woogie	U.S. indie
Bright Star	FRANCE Pathé
Bronson	**UK** Vertigo Films
City Rats	UK *straight to DVD*
Cherrybomb	U.S. indie
Clubbed	UK *straight to DVD*
Creation	**UK** Recorded-Hanway
The Damned United	U.S. Sony Pictures
Doghouse	**UK** Carnaby[23]
Dorian Grey	**UK** Ealing/E1 Ent.
An Education	U.S. Sony Pictures
Endgame	SOUTH AFRICA
Exam	UK *straight to DVD*
Englishman in New York	U.S. indie
Fish Tank	**UK** BBC/Content
FAQ Time Travel	U.S. HBO
Harry Potter and the ½ Blood Prince	U.S. Warner Bros
Hippie Hippie Shake	U.S. & FRANCE
Imaginarium of Dr. Parnassus	U.S. Sony/Infinity
I Know You Know	UK - *not released*
In The Loop	**UK** BBC
Iron Cross	UK *not released*

---

[23] Carnaby is a UK company owned by two L.A.–based Americans. In 2014, it ceased producing and became a distributor.

Is Anybody There	U.S. indie
Jack Boots On Whitehall	U.S. indie
Jack Said	UK *straight to DVD*
Lesbian Vampire Killers	CANADA/Alliance
Little Ashes	U.S. indie
London River	FRANCE
Looking for Eric	FRANCE
Moon	U.S. indie
Nowhere Boy	U.S. Weinstein Corp
Perriers Bounty	IRISH & U.S.
Rage	U.S. indie
Secret of Moonacre	U.S. indie
Sherlock Holmes	U.S. Warner Bros
Shifty	UK BBC - *no release*
St Trinians II	**UK** Ealing Studios
Telstar	NETHERLANDS
Tormented	U.S/FRANCE
Triangle	U.S. indie
Wild Target	**UK** Magic/Protagonist
Young Victoria	U.S. indie

Of the films listed above, 29 weren't British, 4 went straight to DVD, and 3 weren't even released!

Tony Blair, during Prime Minister's Question Time, praised his success in backing British Films by pointing to *Harry Potter*. But *Harry Potter* isn't British. It was made by Warner Bros.

When a Hollywood studio uses British talent to make an American film like *Harry Potter*, it's not a triumph for British films, it's a disaster.

The *Harry Potter* series grossed more than £4.9 billion for Warner Bros. If a British studio had made that money, can you imagine? We'd be back in business.[24]

In 2008, the BBC made *In The Loop* – an intelligent British film.

In the same year, the BBC developed a project called *Tormented,* which they took to two foreign studios, who financed and released it. *Tormented* can't be classified as British because it was financed by Warner Bros and Pathé.

Why did Warners and Pathé fund a project developed by the BBC? Probably because it was a slasher movie, and they thought they'd make some money.

Should the BBC get involved in the Hollywood movie racket? No. When they do, they betray everyone who pays their licence fee.

Tormented illustrates what's known as the 'Calling Card.'

The Calling Card is a British film, made in a Hollywood genre, in the hope that it will get its director noticed in L.A.

Stormy Monday,[25] and *Four Weddings and a Funeral*[26] were Calling Cards. And they both succeeded.

The director of '*Stormy Monday*' was offered work in Hollywood, and the producers of '*Four Weddings*' got a lucrative housekeeping deal with Universal Studios.

---

[24] The Harry Potter film series consisted of 8 movies costing roughly $100 million each. The Tax Credit reimbursed 25% of this, meaning that approximately $200 million – taken from the National Lottery and the British taxpayer – was given to Warner Bros.

[25] Dir: Mike Figgis (Film4/British Screen) 1998

[26] Dir: Mike Newell (Film4/Polygram) 1994

Talented men like Mike Figgis, Eric Fellner and Tim Bevan shouldn't be criticised. They wanted to make films. They couldn't do that in the UK because there are no studios, so they had to go to Hollywood.

British directors, such as Ridley Scott, Tony Scott, Adrian Lyne, Mike Newell, Sam Mendes, Ken Branagh, Bernard Rose, Guy Ritchie, Steven Knight, Matthew Vaughn, David Slade, Jonathan Glazer, Christopher Nolan, and Susanna White all had to go to Hollywood.

Imagine how rich our cinema would be if they worked for us!

So, how do we make films, if there are no British film studios?

With great difficulty is the answer.

Some are made by a TV company, which then sells it to a studio or an independent distributor. Some are made with venture capital (risky) and then offered, via sales companies, to distributors; some are made by pre-selling the film to foreign TV companies and four-walling[27] it at home. Sometimes, self-financed films are made, then submitted to Film Festivals in the hope that a studio will buy it, and others are made by bringing together independent distributors, small investors, and state subsidies, and releasing the film in a handful of arthouse cinemas.

A nation without a movie studio is in danger of losing its identity because our chief medium for reflecting ourselves and our society is movies.

In 1983, Margaret Thatcher abolished the National Film Finance Corporation, the Eady Levy, and the Quota 'in the interests of Free Trade.'

---

[27] Renting cinema screens to exhibit the film yourself.

But is there Free Trade? Hollywood has access to our cinemas, but we don't have access to theirs. Not exactly Free Trade, is it?

US cinemas refuse to show British films unless they're owned by an American distributor. Legally, British companies aren't forbidden from distributing films in the US, but it never happens.

Although, it did happen once:

TIME BANDITS IN AMERICA.

Time Bandits, directed by Terry Gilliam, was made by George Harrison's *Handmade Films* and had a cast including Sean Connery, David Warner, Ian Holm, John Cleese, Michael Palin, Shelly Duvall, and Ralph Richardson.

The film was made for £2m.

Test scores in the US went through the roof. The film was a sure-fire hit and - with the exception of Disney - every Hollywood studio wanted to buy it.

But the studios function as a cartel to pay as little as possible for pick-ups. So, none of them offered more than £2m for the worldwide rights.

HandMade was between a rock and a hard place. If they accepted the £2m, they'd cover their costs but make no profit. If they *didn't* accept the offer, they'd be out of business. So, *HandMade* had no choice. They had to sell to Hollywood.

But they didn't.

George Harrison said: 'Let's go to the States and distribute it ourselves.'

Harrison and his head honcho, Denis O'Brien, went to America, sat down with the major U.S. cinema chains (who all brought their wives to meet the famous Beatle) and talked business.

Despite tremendous goodwill, the U.S. chains regretfully declined to show *Time Bandits* out of fear of what Hollywood might do to them.

Denis O'Brien offered 50% of the receipts for the first two weeks of release – a much better deal than the 10% offered by the Hollywood studios for their films.

But the exhibitors still said no.

Then George Harrison offered to cover their advertising costs. This meant the cinemas would spend nothing. All they had to do was rake in half the cash they took in ticket sales.

This was too good to refuse, so they defied Hollywood and released the film throughout the U.S. - and it was a smash hit.

HandMade made over £10million net profit on the theatrical release – equivalent to about £33million today. And, collectively, the U.S. cinema chains made a lot more than that.

When HandMade finished their next movie, *Privates on Parade,* they called the exhibitors. But they wouldn't even watch the film. Hollywood, enraged by their 'betrayal,' had sworn to bury them if they ever did it again.

Since that time, no British distributor has released a film in the United States. We give America access to our market but are firmly locked out of theirs.

So much for 'Free Trade.'

But you can't blame the businessmen in Hollywood. They're doing what's best for themselves and their shareholders. The villain of the piece is our own Department for International Trade.

Chapter Seven

VIVE LA FRANCE

"We don't have a British film industry, and I'm bored of everyone saying we do have one...We're subsidizing Hollywood. We're service providers. We're not an industry."

Matthew Vaughn [28]

While waiting for the *British Film Institute* to respond to our request for an interview, we wrote to Frédéric Mitterrand, the French Minister of Culture, to ask if we could speak to someone about their film industry.

We received a reply (in French) arranging a meeting with two executives of the *Centre National du Cinema*, in Paris.

The Centre National du Cinema (CNC) is the French equivalent of the British Film Institute.

Kristin Scott Thomas, who often works in France, was quoted as saying she'd turned her back on Hollywood because they didn't provide good roles for women over thirty-five.

They certainly provide good roles for women over thirty-five in France.

If we had our own Cinema in Britain, would we provide good roles for women over thirty-five?

I think we would.

---

[28] Director of *Kick-Ass, X-Men; First Class,* and the *Kingsman* films, in an interview for the BBC series 'The Business of Film.'

Cast your eye over the films we made in the '30s, '40s and '50s, and '60's, and you'll see plenty of good roles for women over thirty-five.

It was a glorious summer's day as we drove towards 12, Rue de Lübeck - the headquarters of the CNC. Robin Dutta, myself, and David Chan, our comrade-in-arms, were eager to see the difference between French and British film bureaucrats.

Once inside the building, we stopped, with our heavy film gear, before a huge baroque staircase, which spiralled upwards.

Michel Plazanet, one of the those we were there to interview, popped his head out to get a God's eye-view of us far below.

Michel Plazanet is the Deputy Director of European and International Affairs. His colleague, Aude Accary-Bonnery, is Deputy Director of Legal and Financial Affairs.

"We support talent.," said Aude Accary-Bonnery "Not someone who just happens to want to make a movie."

Michel and Aude believe the way for French Cinema to prosper is to encourage a wide range of talents and different points of view.

"Ultimately, this is an art. Not just an industry," said Aude.

Michel Plazenet pointed out that their quota system was not to keep Hollywood out, but to ensure a balanced market. They were not against America, but in favour of diversity.

The CNC, which is advised by professionals working in the business, will back anyone who demonstrates ability. Support from the CNC is a vote of confidence that leads to support from studios, TV channels, and banks.

Many French and Belgian co-productions can double up their film tax credits, which helps the producers.

Michel Plazanet told us about their nation-wide youth programmes, where schoolkids watch films in cinemas, not on DVD.

And Aude said: "Un film financé et distribué par Warner Brothers - même s'il avait une histoire française, acteurs français, un établissement français, et a été dans la langue française - ne serait jamais considéré comme un film français, ou d'une partie de notre cinéma national."

("A film financed and distributed by *Warner Bros* – even if it had a French story, French cast, French setting, and was in the French language - would never be regarded as a French film, or part of our national cinema.")

And she added that they were confused by movies billed as British that, when you watched them, seemed to be American.

"Once you start not to protect your Cinema," said Michel Plazenet, "it's finished. Because you can't fight against American power."

We came away feeling that the success of French Cinema was due, for the most part, to the stability of institutions like the CNC, where coherent film policies have evolved.

Not like the UK where the policies never stop chopping and changing.

Chapter Eight

BRITISH CULTURE

"If we tap into stories that are intrinsically English,
we can go on making films till the end of time."

Ken Russell

Britain's history of low culture separates us from the high culture of Europe, where artists were patronised by kings.

The English ruling class - who were not permitted to use their hands in any art or trade - had little time for culture. They preferred hunting, shooting, and fishing.

If a British nobleman needed a painting, he sent his man abroad for a Van Dyke or a Rubens. If a musical concert was required, he hired the services of a Händel or a Haydn. If he wanted a stately home, he sent his man to Italy to copy something.

Culture was left to the commoners.

Ben Johnson's father was a bricklayer, Shakespeare was the son of an alderman, Christopher Marlowe the son of a shoemaker, Thomas Nashe, the son of a curate, Daniel Defoe's dad was a tallow chandler, William Congreve's a soldier, and John Milton's a scrivener - a kind of secretary.

Geoffrey Chaucer, William Blake, John Clare, John Donne, Robbie Burns, Thomas Rowlandson, James Gillray, Jane Austen, Charlotte Bronte, Percy Shelley, John Keats, Samuel Coleridge, Robert Southey, Mary Wollstonecraft, and William Wordsworth were commoners.

Charles Dickens was common. So were Robert Louis Stevenson, Arthur Conan Doyle, W.S. Gilbert and Arthur Sullivan.

Lord Byron was the exception that proves the rule. And he was expelled by his own class.

Our 'low culture' tradition continued into modern times with painters like Francis Bacon, composers like Lennon & McCartney, writers like Ian la Frenais and J K Rowling, and designers like Vivienne Westwood and Alexander McQueen.

Movies were also the creation of commoners, such as Alfred Hitchcock,[29] Edgar Wallace, Sidney Gilliat, and Ronald Neame.

But there were *some* aristocrats who took an interest.

One of these was Anthony Asquith, known to his friends as 'Puffin,' who directed 37 movies. His first: *Shooting Stars*, in 1927, and his last, *The Yellow Rolls Royce*, in 1964.

Winston Churchill was also an upper-class film fan - as was Lady Henrietta Yule, who knew 'everyone,' including King Edward VIII and J. Arthur Rank, the son of a flour baron.[30]

Between 1928 and 1970, popular enthusiasm and aristocratic favour combined to make British Cinema the second biggest film industry in the world.

Carol Reed directed 33 movies. Charles Crichton made 35. Basil Dearden directed 44. Leslie Hiscott made over 60 British films.

In those days, you could have a life-long career in movies without leaving home.

*

---

[29] The second son of William Hitchcock, a greengrocer and poulterer.
[30] Hovis.

Cinema plays a vital role in the life of our nation. We need our own Cinema. If the films we watch are American, we become culturally colonized.

In 1996, Jack Lang, the French Culture Minister, said: "The cultural colonization of France by American films has reached saturation level."

French President, Jacques Chirac said: "I do not want to see European culture sterilized or obliterated by American culture."

If a nation is conquered by force, the conquest isn't permanent because the culture survives. But if a nation is conquered culturally, it's finished – erased.

If we think it's important to defend our culture, we must stop giving our money to Hollywood and invest in our *own* films.

If we made and distributed our own movies, we'd make films with a British sensibility like *I'm All Right Jack*,[31] or *Sir Henry at Rawlinson End*,[32] or *Mr. Turner*. [33]

Since 1983, when the film quota was abolished, nothing's been done to give us access to our screens. Without screens, we cannot have an industry.

When Richard Branson financed *1984* - based on the novel by George Orwell - he had to sell it to MGM to have it released in Britain.

Since the mid-70's, American corporations have controlled almost all our cinemas so, for the past 40 years, we've been steeped in American culture.

Why do we celebrate Halloween? Halloween isn't British. Our

---

[31] Dir: John and Roy Boulting (British Lion) 1959.
[32] Dir: Steve Roberts, (Charisma Records) 1980
[33] Dir: Mike Leigh (Film4) 2014.

Autumn ritual is Bonfire Night.

Why do we have high schools and proms? Why is American football a British sport with a national league and 63 American Football teams? Why do we wear baseball caps?

We don't play baseball.

British shop assistants used to be surly, now they give us fake smiles and say: "Have a nice day!" - a phrase once scorned as ridiculous.

The traditional British attitude to money was disapproving. Doing something for money was reviled. Today, anything you do is okay if you do it for the money.

Another British principle was: 'It's not winning that counts, it's how you play the game.'

Today, no one cares how you play the game, just so long as you win.

These are American – not British values.

Since the early '90s, the American music industry has been selling us gangsters who wear bling, deal drugs, and call their girlfriends bitches and whores. Nothing could be less British. The inhabitants of our apple blossom islands are romantic, inhibited, courteous, and appalled by show-offs.

Fifty years ago, our identities came from our families, our schools, and our local and national cultures. Today, we're not sure of our identities because so many of our models are American.

Sometimes, we might glimpse authentic British characters - in films like *This Is England*,[34] *Kidulthood* [35] and *The Four Lions* [36]

---

[34] Dir: Shane Meadows (Film4) 2007.
[35] Dir: Menhaj Huda (Revolver UK) 2006.
[36] Dir: Chris Morris (Film4) 2010.

– but home-grown movies like these are few and far-between.

In the past, our films gave us British characters in dramas with British themes:

I'm Alright Jack about class conflict; *In Which We Serve* about the Royal Navy; *The Ruling Class* about the aristocracy; the *Doctor* films, the *Carry On* films, *Our Man In Havana*, *Saturday Night and Sunday Morning*, *A Taste of Honey*, *Room At the Top*, *Billy Liar*, *Accident*, *Get Carter*, *Kes*, *The Ipcress File*, and so on.

A list of some of the actors who worked in British films in the 60's illustrates the amazing range of British characters that, back in the day, delighted and enlightened us.

Laurence Olivier	Jimmy Clitheroe
Margaret Rutherford	Richard Harris
Alec Guinness	Dora Bryan
Joyce Grenfell	Tom Courtenay
Hayley Mills	Peter Sellers
Dinsdale Landen	Cyril Cusak
Bernard Miles	Joan Greenwood
Virginia McKenna	Moira Lister
Harry Secombe	Kenneth Williams
Kenneth Connor	Charles Hawtrey
Liz Fraser	Michael Gough
Denholm Elliott	Arthur Askey
Leo McKern	Elke Sommer

Diana Dors	Herbert Lom
Peter Finch	Audrey Hepburn
Christopher Lee	Anthony Newley
Kenneth Haigh	Derek Jacobi
Thora Hird	Peter Cushing
Terry Thomas	John LeMesurier
Dirk Bogarde	Sarah Miles
Sid James	Michael Hordern
Richard Greene	Cecil Parker
Bill Owen	Arthur Kowe
Lionel Jeffries	Hattie Jacques
Donald Pleasance	Robert Newton
Vanessa Redgrave	Donald Wolfit
Michael Caine	Wendy Hiller
Sean Connery	Hazel Court
James Robertson Justice	Paul Scofield
Peter O'Toole	Robert Shaw
Albert Finney	William Franklyn
Patrick Allen	Thorley Walters
Ursula Andress	Shirley-Anne Field
Oliver Reed	Juliet Mills
Fenella Fielding	Joan Hickson
Moira Redmond	Gladys Cooper

Bernard Cribbins

Patrick Wymark

André Morell

Sheila Hancock

John Hurt

Freddie Jones

Dudley Moore

David Warner

Peter Ustinov

Honor Blackman

Harry Andrews

Lesley-Ann Down

Trevor Howard

Nigel Stock

Maxine Audley

Bernard Bresslaw

Tommy Trinder

Eric Porter

David Niven

Gordon Jackson

Richard Attenborough

Michael Wilding

Daniel Massey

Ian Hendry

Douglas Wilmer

Tommy Steele

Wilfred Hyde-White

Richard Burton

James Mason

Jeremy Brett

Kenneth More

Vivien Leigh

Leonard Rossiter

Graham Crowden

Margaret Lockwood

Alan Bates

Dandy Nichols

Richard Griffiths

Malcolm McDowell

Norman Wisdom

Irene Handl

Ronald Fraser

Alfie Bass

Brian Rix

Colin Blakely

Robert Stephens

Geraldine McEwan	Rita Tushingham
Robert Morley	Beryl Reid
Ian Carmichael	Michael York
Rex Harrison	Jack Hawkins
George Cole	Ralph Richardson
Ian Bannen	Nanette Newman
Billie Whitelaw	Stephanie Beacham
Alaister Sim	Ian Ogilvy
Shirley Eaton	Ian McShane
Cardew Robinson	Laurence Harvey
George Formby	Nigel Davenport
Moira Shearer	Wendy Craig
John Gielgud	Julie Ege
Stanley Baker	Coral Browne
Samantha Eggar	Stanley Baxter
Patrick McGoohan	Milo O'Shea
Michael Crawford	Jon Finch
Terence Stamp	Marty Feldman
Anthony Hopkins	Leslie Philips
Tony Hancock	Diane Cilento
Frank Finlay	Gerald Harper
Sylvia Sims	Roy Dotrice
John Gregson	Maurice Denham

Richard Johnson	Thora Hird
Peter Vaughn	Hugh Griffith
Lance Percival	Ian Richardson
Susannah York	Irene Worth
Roger Moore	Sue Lloyd
Michael Bates	Diana Rigg
Edward Fox	Arthur Mullard
James Fox	Peter Cook
Leslie Howard	Charles Laughton

Most of these stars are no longer with us. And, because we have no film industry, they have not been replaced.

When we had our own Cinema, our film stars were our greatest assets, and the lifeblood of our theatre. A West-End show could be financed with one A-list, or two B-list stars.

So, when we lost our cinema, it devastated British Theatre.

Most of all, the passing of our Cinema is the loss of our mirror. Seeing our society represented on screen helped us understand ourselves and the society we live in. Without our own Cinema, we are blind.

We need to see again.

Chapter Nine
THE INTERVIEWS

"Creations of the spirit are not just commodities; the elements of culture are not pure business," proclaimed President François Mitterand. "What is at stake is the cultural identity of all our nations [...] it is the freedom to choose our own images. A society which abandons the means of depicting itself would soon be an enslaved society." In response to the tirade of rhetoric from across the Atlantic, the Europeans pointed out that while Hollywood movies accounted for 80 per cent of box office revenues across much of Europe, films produced in Europe accounted for less than one per cent of the American box office."

David Puttnam

The Undeclared War: Struggle for Control of the World's Film Industry
(HarperCollins 1997)

We went down to London to interview the film director, John Goldschmidt, at his home in Hampstead.

As well as mini-series, documentaries, TV dramas, and music films, Goldschmidt made *Maschenka, Deadly Voyage, The Devil's Lieutenant, A Crime of Honour, Spend, Spend, Spend, Captain Jack, She'll Be Wearing Pink Pyjamas,* and *Dough.*

He's also advised the EU and Channel Four on film policy.

We discussed the state of British Cinema; how the class system organises all human activity in Britain, and how graduates from Oxford and Cambridge universities are appointed to positions in the cultural institutions to guard the establishment.

Another issue that came up was the UK Tax Credit. Any film qualifying as British under the 'Cultural Test,' can get up to 25% of its production budget reimbursed by the British Treasury.

JOHN GOLDSCHMIDT

On the Tax Credit:

"One of the disadvantages of the Tax Credit is it only applies to monies spent inside the UK. That doesn't include the Isle of Man, for example; it doesn't include a co-production shooting on the continent. You couldn't do *The Third Man* and qualify for the UK Tax Credit because it's shot abroad [...] However, the German tax credit allows people working abroad to be claimed against the German tax credit [...] So, the Germans are at a real advantage. It's not a level playing field."

On Sky Television:

"We need Sky Television to be investing in feature films. They have a licence to print money at the moment. They have movie channels. They should be championing British films. They should be doing what the BBC does - but on a bigger scale. They don't want to do it. They have to have their arms twisted. Something has to be done to increase the places we can go – to have a wider range of taste – in what films are made."

On 'The Full Monty':

"Channel Four developed *The Full Monty*, but wouldn't finance it. A man at an American studio – who came from public broadcasting in America and had a brief period at Fox – he fully funded *The Full Monty* when nobody in England would fund it. It became one of the most successful British films of all time.

Channel Four passed, the BBC passed [...] Look at *The King's Speech* – the most successful film of recent times – turned down by Channel Four, turned down by the BBC..."

On the UK Film Council:

"I never really did anything with the Film Council. It was good to have one body representing the film industry as a go-between with the government, and it did lots of interesting things. But it was also crazy to have the British Film Institute and the UK Film Council with all those salaries and administration. It was a dubious crony-world, if you like.

And, when you looked at the Film Council, only 35% of its annual budget was spent on development and production."

*

Sir Ben Kingsley was in London to open a movie in which he plays Georges Méliès – the French film-pioneer – who, flattened by Hollywood, spent his last years selling toys from a kiosk at the Gare Montparnasse.

We asked Ben Kingsley what qualifications the administrators of UK film policy should have.

"They must get down on their knees and say, please [...] walk us through the Powell-Pressburger films, walk us through Noel Coward's *In Which We Serve*... Marinate them in their history."

Ben Kingsley described Cinema as a place of communal light and darkness, where the experience informs, guides and nourishes - a sacred place where all the arts combine to reveal us to ourselves.

He spoke about film as a spiritual, emotional, psychological and intellectual resource that shows us how we cope with our struggles, and how we fall in love.

SIR BEN KINGSLEY

On the Screen Agencies:

If you have people who don't give a damn about film in the film industry, you're sunk. And they *don't* give a damn about film.

On British films:

I don't think British Film has ever tried to outlaw tragedy. There's something in the British that appreciates the world as it truly is – through Shakespeare, through Dickens, through the wonderful composers who wrote for films, like William Walton, or Elgar, or Benjamin Britten...They all had - built into their perspective - light and shade - cause and effect.

To bring you through the narrative, and leave an indelible print on people's imaginations and memories, you've got to have light and shade. It's as basic as black and white.

Now, somewhere along the line, someone's told these gormless executives that people like to be anaesthetized. They were told that people like to – what's the word? – *feel good.*

The more specific you are in the culture of your filmmaking, the more universal your message is.

If you try to generalise your message by setting it in a culture that doesn't really exist, in a time that doesn't really exist, and you soften all the emotional edges so that they don't have a specific cultural root, nobody's touched because everything's so generalised that it's unrecognizable.

You can only empathise with the specific. You cannot empathise with the generalised. And, unfortunately, I think there has been, in the UK, a drift towards material being sent over to us - and created and sold to us - that's been allowed to evolve in such a way, that films are now being made by committee.

And the members of that committee are far more concerned about the parking space of their BMW, and their name on that parking space, than they are with the subtle nuances of a beautiful film.

This is a terrible loss and, sooner or later, people will say: "No, no, no, no, no. We're going to look over here because I can see my life, my struggle, the joy, the beauty of existence [...] I can see it over here. I can't see it over there. What I see over there is anaesthetic.

On Hollywood:

What did Churchill say when he was talking about us and the Americans? 'Divided by a common language.'

So, we mustn't make American films over here.

Americans don't want to see American films made here, anyway. They want to see *British films*! They love our eccentricities. They love this 'thing' that is so English. It's not very good when it gets caricatured, but they love the real thing. They love the real, pure thing. I'm not doing them a disservice. They are our angels. But we must persuade them to take a deep breath and say: "Now, *this* is English."

The French would never outsource their culture. They meet in the Elysée, and redefine and sharpen their language every year. They have a film quota. The French film industry is magnificent. They have an amazing history – starting from Georges Méliès up to today. And we've got to learn our lessons from them. We really have.

Advice to young filmmakers:

I think the new generation of filmmakers have got to be insistent. They've got to get their message across aggressively that they are the defenders of our culture; that they are the new poets of our civilisation. And I think they have to get rid of the naysayers, and the people who 'tut' and shake their heads.

And they have to be courageous, and *not* self-deprecating. Know that they are of great worth to our culture and of great worth to the audience – and of great worth to the beauty and longevity of film.

I met David Lean very late on in his life. It was at a gathering of Brits who'd won Academy Awards at a most amazing venue – Windsor Castle. You can imagine the smell of self-deprecation that was seeping into the tapestry.

And I met David Lean...I was thrilled to meet him...and I told him, in no uncertain terms, whilst shaking his hand, how much I admired his work and how thrilling it was to meet him.

"Yes," was his answer. "Yes."

I thought: 'Good for you. That's the way to do it!'

So far, we've screened *Who Killed British Cinema?* in Cannes, London and Birmingham. Each time, audiences were gripped when Ben Kingsley was onscreen, and what he said launched many passionate discussions afterwards.

*

Lord David Puttnam made the movies we'd grown up with. I'd tracked his career from *Stardust* through to becoming chairman of Columbia Pictures, and devoured his seminal work: *The Undeclared War - Struggle for Control of the World's Film Industry.*

LORD DAVID PUTTNAM

On Corruption:

I never really encountered any direct corruption. Although I did encounter *silly* bits of corruption – such as over BAFTA awards - when people weren't quite kosher.

On Cultural Bureaucrats:

The idea that people stay in those privileged positions for more than five years is, to me, anathema. That's the mistake: when people move into a cultural position and then turn it into a career...it's not supposed to be a career; it's supposed to be a stepping-stone. They ought to be out *making* films.

I'm not remotely interested in paying people's mortgages as a result of making decisions about cultural expenditure. That's wrong. And I've never wavered from that belief.

On the Eady Levy:

What was catastrophic was killing off the Eady Fund. The Eady Fund was absolutely fundamental. I put Eady money into three of my first four films. It wasn't huge. It was about 20% - 25%, in some cases. Ridley Scott's first film was Eady money.

Alan Parker's first film was Eady money.

On Government:

Government needs to decide how important it sees not only the film industry but the creative industries generally. Is it going to look at them as something needing to be protected or as things to be thrown to the wolves – be those wolves *News Corp, Sky,* or *Google*? That's a political judgement. There's no way of knowing at the moment which way that will go.

In a sense, this is where I lose the plot because, quite deliberately, in 1998, I joined the Department of Education rather than stay within the DCMS[37] and deal with film policy. So, what went on from 1998 onwards, was off the radar for me.

The main question is: where are we on the pecking order? Financial Services can walk in and out of Downing Street whenever they want to. We've discovered that News Corp can walk in and out of Downing Street whenever they want to. It is certainly not the case that the film industry can walk in and out whenever it wants to.

The important thing is that if Amanda Nevill[38] and Greg Dyke[39] do walk through the doors, are they being listened to? Are they respected? Are they coming up with policies that are saleable and affordable?

If the answer is 'yes,' then things could be quite good. If the answer is 'no,' we're back in the doldrums."

Puttnam told a story he'd heard from John Major who, when he was Foreign Secretary, visited the USA and sat down with his counterpart, the U.S. Secretary of State, James Baker.

---

[37] Department for Culture, Media and Sport.
[38] Chief Executive of the British Film Institute.
[39] Chairman of the British Film Institute (2008 - 2016.)

James Baker snapped at him: "What are you trying to do to our film industry?"

John Major was utterly baffled.

With this story, Puttnam was illustrating Hollywood's importance to the American government, and British Cinema's *lack* of importance to the British government.

*

Mike Hodges has done extensive TV and documentary work, and his feature films include: *Get Carter, Pulp, Flash Gordon,* and *Croupier.*

When we asked people to name their favourite British film, *Get Carter* was the most often mentioned.

Hodges's introduction to cinema came, at the age of 15, when he skipped school to watch a film crew shooting nearby. He recognized the actors - David Niven and the Midlands-born Margaret Leighton - but wasn't aware he was seeing Michael Powell and Emeric Pressburger making *The Elusive Pimpernel.*

He told us his film, *Croupier,* a local story, starring the then-unknown Clive Owen, was a surprise hit in America.

Bought by an independent U.S. distributor named *Shooting Gallery,* it ran for eight months in 117 movie theatres.

This corroborates Ben Kingsley's statement that: "Americans don't want to see American films being made in the UK, they want to see British films."

Hodges also remarked that foreign control of our distribution always posed an obstacle for directors like him.

"If I'd lived in France or America, I probably would've made a film a year."

MIKE HODGES

On Current Filmmaking:

"I think there are too many references to other films. People like me had an advantage, in an odd sort of way, because we only saw a film once. I only ever saw Billy Wilder's or John Huston's films once. So, whilst you would absorb it like a sponge, you couldn't copy it. But now you have VHS and DVDs and you can run them time and time again. So, of course, they become deeply ingrained and you can't help but copy them.

Too many filmmakers these days make derivative dross. Although, if you're working for a powerful cartel that controls distribution, even derivative dross can make money."

On Hollywood Films:

"I have absolutely no desire to see any of them. I truly don't. None of those films interest me. They're too sentimental, and I hate feeling manipulated.

When you have David Cameron (UK Prime Minister) making speeches about how we need to support blockbusters, it's just drivel. Utter drivel. But then he probably only watches films like 'The King's Speech' or – ugh! – 'Notting Hill.'"

On Government Screen Agencies:

"Bureaucracies are curious things. Talk about 'Nature filling a vacuum' - these organisations seem to do just that - and for nice, healthy salaries!"

On Film Policy:

"There was an absolutely great period of Australian filmmaking, with 'Picnic at Hanging Rock,' 'Mad Max,' and a whole range of different films that were, somehow, financed with help from the Australian government. In ten years, the whole world's conception of Australia was transformed. Successive governments in the UK have never understood that our country's identity has not come across on film."

Advice to young filmmakers:

"Part of me says: 'Don't attempt it because it's so tough.' The other part says: 'Encourage and hope for the best.' You can only really encourage - but temper it by telling the facts."

Hodges also said something disturbing about today's audiences. He said they'd been manipulated so thoroughly by Hollywood, that many of them now felt uncomfortable watching a film with a British sensibility.

*

Director/producer Tony Klinger began directing in the late 1960's, for ATV television, before line-producing his first feature: *Shout At the Devil,* starring Roger Moore.[40] Further features, TV series, documentaries, and music videos followed. He also became a media consultant, film course leader, and university lecturer.

TONY KLINGER

On Hollywood:

We're the country that actually made *Superman, Alien, Star Wars* – everything like that – but all that money goes overseas.

---

[40] Roger Moore regarded this as his best film.

Would it not be common sense for our bankers and money guys to say: 'We'll make some *Aliens* and *Star Wars* because they make billions of dollars for those companies in America?'

But no, we won't make those, we'll let the Americans do that, and we'll give them an incentive to come here."

On British Films:

The thing that we're good at is writing. It goes back to Chaucer, Shakespeare, and Dickens. We're better than most other countries in the world – per capita, certainly.

We've got fantastic directors. We have wonderful creative talents – all negated by one thing: we don't have sufficient creative producers – entrepreneurial men and women who have an international feel for doing the business of making films.

Instead, what's happened in the UK is we've trained a whole generation to be great at form-filling.

So now we have producers who aren't producers because they don't know how to raise real money. And if you don't know how to raise real money, you don't know how to spend real money. And if you don't know how to spend real money, how can you market? And if you don't know about marketing, you don't know about sales, and if you don't know about sales, you don't know about distribution.

And if you don't know about distribution, you certainly don't know about exhibition."

*

Next, we were lucky enough to interview the impresario Michael Kuhn.

Michael Kuhn set up PolyGram Filmed Entertainment in 1991 and, over the next eight years, established the only British based film studio - with operations in 14 countries and revenues of $1 billion. He also set up PolyGram Television, produced several successful dramas and series, and founded PolyGram Specialist Video, which became one of the top five sell-through companies in the world.

MICHAEL KUHN

Ex-President of PolyGram Filmed Entertainment

On British Films:

The profits come from distribution so, if you don't have access to distribution, you can't have a sustainable film industry.

And you need marketing. You can only have a success if you market your way to success. It doesn't happen by itself.

The government, for political reasons, are never going to force Sky, the BBC, or Channel Four to invest in British films. That will never happen. Read my lips.

On the Eady Levy:

I think the Eady Levy was fabulous. It supported not only British filmmakers but other things, like the Children's Film Foundation, which collapsed when it was abolished. But that was then and this is now.

On Screen Agencies:

I've always felt that any government film agency should – no matter how great the challenge – have a go at setting up a sustainable film industry. The UK Film Council had a go at the beginning. They had the right idea but they gave up too soon.

They had 'slate deals' with various groups of producers. But because it wasn't an immediate success, after 3 years, they gave up and washed their hands of it. And I think this put them off ever doing it again, which is a pity.

...I think one of the problems we have in the UK is the establishment practice of advertising for jobs that are already filled. When you see a job advertised - such as the Governor of the BBC - you'd be an idiot to apply because it's already been arranged who the Governor's going to be. But they have to go through a 'due process' to make it seem democratic.

This still goes on today, without very good results.

On the Lord Smith Report:

I'm a big fan of his. He's one of the best arts ministers we've had. But all politicians do 'management-speak.' It's easy to say words people will vote for. "I'm in favour of the audience."

Well, I'm in favour of the audience too.

"I'm against evil."

Well, so am I.

"I'm in favour of good."

I'm definitely in favour of good!"

*

We made our way to Westminster to interview Sir Gerald Kaufman M.P.

Gerald Kaufman had been a Labour minister, Shadow Home Secretary, Shadow Foreign Secretary, Chairman of the *Culture,*

Media and Sport Select Committee, and chairman of the *Booker Prize* judges.

Kaufman is also a film buff who believes British films should not lose their national passport.

In the 1990s he criticized *Four Weddings and A Funeral* on the grounds that it traduced our national identity by having been made for the American market and slanted to flatter Americans.

"The celluloid never-never land we were shown for 117 minutes bore no resemblance to what goes on in this island of ours."

SIR GERALD KAUFMAN M.P.

"It was a very good thing in this country – just as it was in the United States – to have a vertically integrated structure. And in the case of Rank, well, the Rank Organisation not only made the films but also owned the distribution, and the Odeon and Gaumont cinema chains - so there was an assured outlet for their films. The American courts decided this was not a good thing. I think the American courts were wrong."

..."UK film policy has too much structure and not enough vision. Vision should lead and structure follow – not the other way round."

..."The multiplexes are foolish in preventing audiences from seeing smaller films."[41]

---

[41] The cogency of this view was demonstrated when, in 2014, the multiplexes lost money by underestimating demand for Mike Leigh's '*Mr Turner,*' starring Timothy Spall.

..."There's too much media coverage of movies based on Marvel and DC comics... British journalists should not support Hollywood action films rather than original cinema."

We discussed the government's last film initiative: *The Lord Smith Report,* which was released in January 2012.

Commissioned by Culture Minister, Ed Vaizey, the Report, after a very lengthy consultation period - was published with 56 recommendations for improving conditions for British films and filmmakers.

Sir Gerald believed Lord Smith made some good points, but the report did not address the following:

1. A Film Quota.

2. The lack of British film studios.

3. The tax credit system that promotes foreign productions at the expense of British productions.

4. Rupert Murdoch's Sky TV licence, which mandates no support for British filmmakers.

5. Restoration of the Eady Levy, to help British producers.

6. The Virtual Print Fee, which penalizes British films.

7. The BBC's limited investment in British films.

8. The lack of a dedicated movie channel on terrestrial television.

Unfortunately, with another meeting for the MP to attend, we had to cut our interview short.

(Sadly, in February 2017, the Right Honourable Sir Gerald Kaufman passed away. He will be very sorely missed.)

*

Lord Smith's report came up in our next interview too, with another man named Smith - the highly successful British producer, Iain Smith OBE. His long list of credits includes:

Local Hero, starring Burt Lancaster

The Mission, starring Robert de Niro

Hearts of Fire, starring Bob Dylan

Killing Dad, starring Richard E. Grant

City of Joy, starring Patrick Swayze

1492, starring Gerard Depardieu

Mary Reilly, starring Julia Roberts

The Fifth Element, starring Bruce Willis

Seven Years in Tibet, starring Brad Pitt

Entrapment, starring Sean Connery

Spy Game, starring Robert Redford

Cold Mountain, starring Jude Law

Alexander, starring Colin Farrell

The Fountain, starring Hugh Jackman

IAIN SMITH OBE

On the Loss of British Cinema:

"Rank and ABPC made completely the wrong choices. They owned a full network of cinemas throughout this country.

Back in the early '60's, there was an opportunity to stabilise that and build a vertically integrated industry, but they closed down cinemas and turned them into bowling alleys and dance halls.

So, we saw the end of the opportunity for the creative side of the industry to have an outlet to a paying market."

On the Lord Smith Report:[42]

"The Tax Credit is a great thing. Without it, our film industry would cease to exist. So, we need to have it. But it's been set up in a less than great way. But the government specifically disallowed us from discussing the Tax Credit."

On the British Film Institute:

"They've always been a reactive organisation, in my view. Now they need to become pro-active.

They're going to have to change the world, not just understand it.

They can do that in terms of local distribution within the UK – encouraging more independent cinemas, and adopting more of the 'Cinèmateque' approach - which the French have had for decades - and encouraging audience awareness of the full range of movies on offer."

*

Stephen Frears was in post-production on *Muhammad Ali's Greatest Fight,* starring Christopher Plummer and Frank Langella. Our meeting took place early in the morning, to fit in with his editing schedule.

We asked him how he would define a British film.

---

[42] Iain Smith was a panelist on the Lord Smith enquiry.

"Who gives a monkey's?"

"If we had a quota, could a British book like *High Fidelity* [43] be shot in London with a British cast?"

"Why would you need a quota for that?"

"If you could have a good script, or a guaranteed release date, which would you rather have?"

"You sound like Tony Richardson."

Many regard Frears as Britain's best movie director. [44]

STEPHEN FREARS

On British Films:

I would have great trouble talking about the modern British Cinema. I read these things about what a triumph it is and I think, well, I can see *Fish Tank* was a very good film, but I'm not sure what the other good ones were.

On Screen Agencies:

I was on the board of a Screen Agency [45] but I never gave myself any money. What a fool I was!

The UK Film Council was, I think, set up in the wrong way.

On Making Films:

If you're middle-class, you're privileged. I went to Trinity because my father went to Trinity. I don't remember being

---

[43] An American comedy-drama directed by Frears, based on the novel by Nick Hornby, with the setting moved from London to Chicago.

[44] His films include: *Gumshoe, My Beautiful Laundrette, Dangerous Liaisons, Prick Up Your Ears, The Grifters, Dirty Pretty Things, The Queen, Philomena, Florence Foster Jenkins,* and *Victoria and Abdul.*

[45] He was on the board of EM Media - maybe one reason they were so effective.

interviewed or anything like that. I read Law, which was an unimaginative choice on my part. So, I don't present that as an achievement.

Is it a flat playing field?

No. Has it ever been a flat playing field? No.

Things got worse when Thatcher came in. Mrs Thatcher caused chaos. She wasn't a good Prime Minister. You now can see that clearly.

Blair wasn't a good Prime Minister.

All the trouble in the economy goes back to them. They brought in these dreadful values.

Advice for Young Filmmakers:

I don't know. It must be very, very tough being young. We thought we had it hard, but we didn't. We had it easy.

QUESTION: What did you learn from Karel Reisz and Lindsay Anderson?

They were both very fine men. And they were intelligent men. And they were very committed men - and very sophisticated. They were Europeans. And it was very interesting to sit at their feet and learn about the world.

I remember Jack Clayton - who was to one side of that gang - saying to me, after I'd made *Gumshoe*: "Don't be like us. Don't wait five years to make your next film."

And Lindsay used to say: "Go and make a 'B' movie" or "Go and make a cop film!"

He was always full of praise for people who did that – although he never did it himself!

Listen, to have people as inspiring as that around is good for anybody. Is the world like that now? No.

Can I change the world? No. I've failed."

A year later, BAFTA nominated his film, *Philomena,* for 'Most Outstanding British Film.'

But the award went to *Gravity.*

We wondered if his reaction was the same as ours: "Hey! *Gravity* is <u>not</u> a British film!"

*

Our next interview was with Ken Loach.

I asked him why there'd been such a gap between *Looks and Smiles,* (1981) and his political thriller about Northern Ireland, *Hidden Agenda* (1990).

"The '80s were disastrous for Britain - due to Thatcherism. I fought back by making activist documentaries that were a waste of time because they were all banned.[46]

It was a terrible time.

Believe it or not, Channel Four used to advertise for 'right-wing thinking' producers!"

We asked if he'd been invited to be on the Lord Smith Panel of Advisors to Government on Film Policy (which included Julian Fellowes and Iain Smith OBE).

"No. Obviously, Fellowes is a Tory, and they wouldn't want me because they know I'd disagree."

---

[46] *The Gamekeeper* and *A Question of Leadership* are now available on Ken Loach's YouTube channel.

KEN LOACH

Advice to young people:

The people who make films are, by and large, not directors. There are many trades and many crafts and many people involved. And there are a certain number of people who will find work.

A far greater number of people will be turned out by colleges and media courses and film schools who will never find work.

Some of them will go into teaching and then it becomes a whole empty spiral of people talking about something they haven't actually done. And I think that's bad because it's a hollow process.

Much better to study English History, or languages, or economics – something with real content.

So, would I recommend young people to go into the business? Well, if you've got a passion for it, and you've got a skill, then give it a shot. But have the back door open so you can do something else.

On British films:

Many films made in Britain, by largely British technicians, come from the American culture. So, we service American films.

For something to be British, it has to come from our culture - from our sensibilities, from our experience, from our way of looking at the world - from our sense of humour.

To have a colonial invader park himself in Pinewood and then say he's made a British film is nonsense.

On the Eady Levy:

Of course, the Americans don't want it – and the big international corporations who control the cinemas don't want it - because it would take a little of their profit.

On the Quota:

Quotas are good in a bad system. If you're going to stick with the way cinemas are currently owned and programmed, then they need to be disciplined by saying: 'well, you've got to show a certain proportion of world cinema, European cinema and British cinema in order to ensure that the audience has got a range of films.' The market doesn't provide that.

The market is an inefficient mechanism that produces monopolies. That's the name of the game.

I think that for things to really work, we have to change the pattern of ownership. Have cinemas programmed by people who care about films – not by people who care about fast food.

The whole system is corrupt. You need to start again. We need a new economic model.

Creative England and the BFI adopt the tired language of old business schools. You read their grotty - I mean glossy - brochures, and lose the will to live...

We've been culturally colonised. It's something we need to resist - and to do that is political.

It's not only in cinema, it's in every aspect of our daily life. It's in our foreign policy, which is maybe more important.

Bombing Iraq at the behest of the Yanks is probably rather more important than what they're doing to our cinema.

So, I think it's a much bigger problem than just within cinema. Grappling with that is part of what you have to do in order to understand what films you want to make.

You can't see filmmaking in isolation. It's part of our political history.

Why are we dominated by the United States?

To understand that, you have to see the whole broad picture, and then work out how to fight back.

As the man said: 'It's not just to understand it, it's to change it.'

*

Our final interview was with film director Sir Alan Parker.

Parker directed *Bugsy Malone* (1976), *Fame* (1980), *Pink Floyd - The Wall* (1982), *The Commitments* (1991), *Evita* (1996), *Midnight Express* (1978), *Shoot the Moon* (1982), *Angel Heart* (1987), *Mississippi Burning* (1998), *Come See the Paradise* (1990), *Angela's Ashes* (1999), and *The Life of David Gale* (2003).

"American films dominate our cinema because that's what the audience wants to see."

He gave the example of *Sunshine On Leith,*[47] released by *Entertainment Film Distributors*.[48]

"The film was able to get into cinemas in the UK but didn't do well because the audience didn't respond to a film made in Glasgow. My argument to you is: will they come? The Curzon[49] has a very hard time [...] Lenin, Stalin and Hitler saw cinema as

---

[47] Dir Dexter Fletcher, starring Peter Mullan and Jane Horrocks. (BFI) 2013.
[48] A laudable British distribution company owned and operated by Trevor and Nigel Green.
[49] The Curzon is a small cinema chain showing independent films.

propaganda but the audiences didn't give a toss about that. They wanted to watch Fred Astaire."

He dismissed our notion that there might be a political will to suppress British Cinema.

"Politicians are more worried about television than cinema because television reaches a wider audience. Film has never had an effect on the political classes."

SIR ALAN PARKER

On the Screen Agencies:

"We've been through this argument where you sit round a table, with all the film industry people represented, and you put your hand up and say: 'Excuse me, I think all the money should go to new people."

And they all go: "Bugger off! What about me? I've got a mortgage as well!"

..."The BFI are a passive administration that panders to the status quo. They're not going to change anything."

Advice to Young People:

"Be wary," I would say to young people.

It's hard, but because it's hard, that's why it's so satisfying to succeed within it. Because, to be able to make a great movie with all of those difficulties, is an enormous achievement - when you think about how hard it is.

To be able to write it in the first place - to create it, to beg for the money to get it made, to fight for the film that you want to make, and then, ultimately, for an audience to go and see it, and for it to be a success... All of those things – to get them all right –

anyone who's done that, I take my hat off to them because so many people don't succeed is the truth.

On the Eady Levy:

The Eady Levy was a way in which the successful films – which were primarily American – would contribute to an indigenous film industry, so we would not be swamped by American production.

That was the reason behind it all. And it worked pretty well. That money went back into the film industry and allowed a lot of people to make their own British films with a British voice.

I suppose I was just at the end of that really because it all went a bit doolally the moment they got rid of the Eady Levy.

I know we all suffered when it went.

On Hollywood:

They're only interested in one thing, the Americans – money.

The whole of British Cinema has been corrupted by big-budget American films. That's all the audiences have got used to watching. And, therefore, their intellect, their sensibility, their attention span has all declined, and it's harder and harder to get an intelligent film to be successful.

On The Lord Smith Report:

The whole of that report was rubbish. It did nothing. I don't know when it was published, but nothing's been done. No one's acted upon it whatsoever. So, what's the point of it?

The only reason to analyse – which his group was supposed to do – is to effect change. But they didn't effect anything – not for one tiny second did anything change.

So, what's the point of it? Lord Smith or anybody – it doesn't matter - he's not a filmmaker anyway. He's a politician.

Nothing happened. Nothing!"

Chapter Ten
WHO KILLED BRITISH CINEMA?

"The nine scariest words in the English language are:
'I'm from the Government and I'm here to help.'"

Ronald Reagan

By 1970, British Cinema was in trouble. Television was taking its audience, and revenues had dropped like a stone.

The figures speak for themselves.

In 1946, cinema admissions were 1,635 million. By 1972 they'd fallen to 156.6 million - a drop of over 90%.

Hollywood was having the same trouble so, desperate for every dollar, it banned British film distributors from the US market. This was in violation of the *General Agreement on Tariffs and Trade,* but they did it anyway. (See: *Time Bandits In America* - page 75.)

Panic set in, and the bosses at Associated British Pictures, The Rank Organisation and British Lion cut production, sold off assets, and diversified.

Hollywood pounced on their devalued assets and MGM, United Cinemas International, National Amusements Inc., and Warner Theatres bought up 80% of Britain's cinemas.

'The Monopolies and Merger Commission's Report of 1995 discovered that 'all the leading exhibitors except Odeon have some ownership link, direct or indirect, with a Hollywood studio' (Report on the Supply of Films for Exhibition in Cinemas in the UK: Summary 1.3.)'

British National Cinema, by Sarah Street.
(Routledge 2009).

Why didn't our studio bosses go to the government for help?

Well, they did, and, in 1970, Edward Heath, the Prime Minister, roundly declared that British Cinema was 'in the public interest.'

However, later that year, the National Film Finance Corporation's annual credit line was reduced from £6m to £1m and - three years later - to a paltry £500,000.

The world's second biggest film industry was heading for extinction.

The UK government made no provision to save its national film industry and, as previously stated, in 1983, Margaret Thatcher abolished the National Film Finance Corporation, the Eady Levy, and our indispensable film quota.

Franklin D. Roosevelt once said: "Nothing in politics ever happens by accident. If it happens, you can bet it was planned that way."

If true, it means the UK Film Council was intentionally set up to encourage Hollywood films to be made and distributed in Britain – thus destroying British Cinema.

The inexperience of those appointed to run the Regional Screen Agencies (with the exception of EM Media) must also have been intentional. Experienced filmmakers were available, but not approached.

When a detective begins a murder enquiry, he will see if anyone's tried to cover it up. Anyone covering up a murder is likely to be involved in it.

Did anyone try to cover up the murder of British Cinema?

Here's what Lord Chris Smith, the Culture Minister, said in January 2012, when the official UK market share of British films was a mere 5.5% (it was certainly less.)

"British film is going through a golden period. A run of British-made and British-based movies has been taking audiences around the world by storm. But we cannot be complacent - this review highlights the things that the BFI, Government and industry can do to ensure that we continue to build on recent successes. British film is in prime position to make a major contribution to the growth of the UK's economy, to the development of attractive and fulfilling careers for young people and to the creation of job opportunities across the country."

This false statement is a cover-up.

So, who killed British Cinema? Well, clearly, it was our own government.

But why did they do that? And why do they continue to block attempts to revive it?

At one time, social engineering was the task of the Church. Today, it's the job of the education system and the media.

By the end of the 19th Century, our rulers understood the importance of the media. So, when films, radio, and television were invented, they made sure to control them.

Government declared ownership of the airwaves and ordered radio and TV broadcasters to obtain (and pay for) 'licences.' These licences, which were limited, and had to be renewed, could be swiftly withdrawn if the broadcaster stepped out of line.

Films weren't so easy to control. The only tool was censorship, which stirs rebellion.

For most people, films were more appealing than radio or television because of their greater freedom of thought. It was this freedom of thought that made film our foremost cultural medium.

In the 1960's, British films began to express anti-establishment ideas. As Frederic Raphael[50] said:

"The governed no longer accepted as gospel the virtues once attributed to their governors and established institutions."

To make matters worse, the new movie stars were working class. No-one had seen actors like Albert Finney, Richard Burton, Diana Dors, Sean Connery, Terence Stamp, and Michael Caine in leading roles before.

Did this upsurge in working class confidence deter the government from supporting British Cinema?

---

[50] Writer of *Darling* (1965), *Two For The Road* (1967), *The Glittering Prizes* (1976), *Eyes Wide Shut* (1999).

Chapter Eleven

THE QUOTA

'If an industry is understood to mean something that supplies continuity of production and employment, Britain has no film industry.'

Geoffrey Macnab
'J Arthur Rank and The British Film Industry'
(Routledge)

"Once, we had a British film industry that rivalled the best of Hollywood, from serious drama to comedy. And we had British directors [...] and stars, who were internationally acclaimed.

Why? Because British filmmaking was protected by a quota.

But it all came to an end on 1 January 1983, when Margaret Thatcher scrapped it.

Since then we've become a country where the film industry has gone the same way as the car industry: we build Japanese cars, and we make films for Hollywood studios – so long as we give them big enough cash incentives, that is.

British filmmaking has been reduced to a cottage industry where filmmakers have the option of either making films on virtually no money, or on small budgets with grants from the National Lottery. And these films only end up in our mainstream cinemas if Hollywood acquires them – and pockets most of the money.

It's hardly surprising then that 19 out of 20 of these truly British films loses money.

The quota was first introduced in 1928, and by 1935, 20% of

all films that were distributed and exhibited in the UK, had to be British.

On top of this, the 1960 Film Act made it illegal for distributors to force exhibitors to take films they didn't want by bundling films together so that cinemas could only have the latest blockbuster if they took the studio's other films as well.

Margaret Thatcher scrapped this too; which is why - today - British cinemas (exhibitors) can't get the new 'Star Wars' unless they take 6 other unpopular films by the same studio. Now you know why our multiplexes are clogged with bad American films.

The scrapping of quotas has proved a disaster in other countries as well. For example, in 1992, as part of the North American Free Trade Agreement, Mexico abolished its quota. This led to a collapse of Mexican cinema, with production falling from more than 100 features per year down to single figures. In an attempt to save the industry, the Mexican government reintroduced a 10% quota in 1997.

South Korea first introduced a film quota (10%) in 1967 - then progressively raised it to effectively 40% by 1985. The result was an industry in which South Korean films regularly outstrip the biggest Hollywood blockbusters at the box office, and which has survived the halving of the quota, under US free trade pressure, in 2006.

Other examples include the re-emergence of both Spanish and Latin American cinema, France's continuing significance, and, one could even argue, the US itself, where Hollywood's control of the North American market effectively adds up to a 95%+ quota...

It's only quotas that will give British films and distributors a fair crack of the whip. Without them, we will simply continue to throw Lottery money away on films that, no matter how good they may be, have virtually no chance of being shown outside London."

Jon Williams.[51]

Today, less than 12 British features are released each year. But, if 20% of the UK market were ring-fenced for British films, that would change very quickly.

The government can do this with a stroke of the pen. The state already maintains a quota of 60% on British terrestrial television. (60% of what's broadcast on TV must be financed by British companies.) So, there's no reason not to apply the same principle to British films.

Perhaps now - with Britain becoming free of the EU – there'll be an appetite to reassert our own cultural identity?

Multi-culturalism has failed – as it was bound to do – because it drowns national identity in a swamp of foreign identities.

Put simply, multi-culture means 'no culture.'

That's not to say we should cut ourselves off from other cultures, as Japan once did. Cultures benefit greatly from contact with one another, but only if they maintain their own cultural integrity.

So, let us be ourselves again - and celebrate ourselves again. And, to help us do it, let's rebuild our film industry.

All we need is a quota.

When we have a quota, we won't need subsidies, grants, bursaries, tax credits, or Lottery money.

British Cinema was established without public money and, in spite of the Entertainment Tax, prospered and grew. And, when threatened by Hollywood, it was saved by a film quota.

---

[51] Journalist and author

It worked well then and it will work well now.

The reason most countries have film quotas is culture. Their governments think their national culture is in the national interest. And it *is*. After all, what is a nation? It's territory, its language, and its culture.

Sweden has a 14% quota and, despite fierce competition from Hollywood, regularly achieves a healthy 26% share of its domestic market.

In 2008, Sweden released 37 films including *Let The Right One In,* and *The Girl With the Dragon Tattoo.* In 2009, the Swedish Film Institute celebrated 145 International awards given to Swedish films.

Argentina has an 8.3% film quota. In 2008, Argentina released 23 new movies. This compares to only 9 British films released in the UK in the same year (See: pages 71-72).

From 1983 to the present, Great Britain - a nation of officially 64.6million – has released an average of 11 films a year. Denmark, a nation of 5.6million has averaged 29 films per year over the same time-period.

Why is Denmark doing better than us? Because it has a 12% quota.

France protects approximately 15% of its domestic market for French films. Since 1970, this policy, combined with subsidies, has enabled France to release, on average, 102 French movies each year.

France's population, at 64.9 million, is almost the same as ours, so it's reasonable to assume that, with the same quota and subsidies, we'd soon have a flourishing industry like the French.

People old enough to remember when we made our own films, might tell you they weren't good - that the Hollywood films were better. This is what the French say about French films today.

I've even heard Frenchmen say the quota should be scrapped to 'force the filmmakers to make better films.' This is nuts. If the quota was removed, French Cinema would collapse.

To make 5 good films a year, you need to make 50 films. Most movies don't succeed. It's the same in the book industry and the music industry. When you buy an album of twelve songs, how many of the songs are good? Maybe two or three.

The important thing is to make those 50 films a year.

Since the loss of *PolyGram* in 1998, Britain has not had a single movie studio.

Look at what Ken Loach had to endure to make *The Wind That Shakes the Barley*. Deals had to be made with 17 different companies.

Sixteen Films

Matador Pictures

Regent Capital

The UK Film Council

Bord Scannan na Héireann

Element Films

BIM Distribuzione

EMC Produktion

Tornasol Films

Diaphana Films

Pathé

Cinéart

TV3 Television Network Ireland

Irish Film Board

Oil Flick Films No.2

Filmcoopi Zurich

Filmstiftung-Nordrhein-Westfalen

And to get it to the public, the film had to be sold to 22 separate distributors. What a hassle!

Let's have a 20% quota. With access to 20% of our screens, investing in British films becomes viable, and our films can pay their way. There's no shortage of talent to make them.

We used to have the second biggest film industry in the world and, with a 20% quota, we can have that again.

We deserve it.

We deserve to celebrate ourselves and our culture again.

The End.

A Must-See List of British Films

Blackmail (1929)
Dir Alfred Hitchcock (Anny Ondra, Sara Allgood, John Longden)

A Cottage on Dartmoor (1929)
Dir Anthony Asquith (Hans Adalbert von Schlettow, Uno Henning, Norah Baring)

Piccadilly (1929)
Dir EA Dupont (Anna May Wong, Gilda Gray, Jameson Thomas)

The 39 Steps (1935)
Dir Alfred Hitchcock (Robert Donat, Madeleine Carroll, Godfrey Tearle)

Sabotage (1936)
Dir Alfred Hitchcock (Oscar Homolka, Sylvia Sidney, John Loder)

The Lady Vanishes (1938)
Dir Alfred Hitchcock (Margaret Lockwood, Michael Redgrave)

Went the Day Well? (1942)
Dir Alberto Cavalcanti (Leslie Banks, Elizabeth Allan, Frank Lawton)

A Canterbury Tale (1944)
Dirs Michael Powell, Emeric Pressburger (Eric Portman, Sheila Sim, John Sweet, Dennis Price)

Brief Encounter (1945)
Dir David Lean (Trevor Howard, Celia Johnson)

Dead of Night (1945)
Dirs Alberto Cavalcanti, Charles Crichton, Basil Dearden, Robert Hamer (Mervyn Johns, Michael Redgrave, Roland Culver)

I Know Where I'm Going! (1945)
Dirs Michael Powell, Emeric Pressburger (Wendy Hiller, Roger Livesey)

Great Expectations (1946)
Dir David Lean (John Mills, Valerie Hobson, Martita Hunt)

A Matter of Life and Death (1946)
Dirs Michael Powell, Emeric Pressburger (David Niven, Kim Hunter, Roger Livesey, Raymond Massey)

It Always Rains on Sunday (1947)
Dir Robert Hamer (Googie Withers, Edward Chapman, John McCallum)

The Fallen Idol (1948)
Dir Carol Reed (Ralph Richardson, Michèle Morgan, Bobby Henry

Whisky Galore! (1949)
Dir Alexander Mackendrick (Basil Radford, Joan Greenwood, Jean Cadell)

The Third Man (1949)
Dir Carol Reed (Joseph Cotten, Orson Welles, Alide Valli)

Kind Hearts and Coronets (1949)
Dir Robert Hamer (Dennis Price, Alec Guinness, Joan Greenwood)

The Ladykillers (1955)
Dir Alexander Mackendrick (Alec Guinness, Peter Sellers, Katie Johnson)

The Bridge on the River Kwai (1957)
Dir David Lean (Alec Guinness, William Holden, Jack Hawkins)

Dracula (1958)
Dir Terence Fisher (Peter Cushing, Christopher Lee, Michael Gough)

I'm Alright Jack (1959)
Dir John Boulting (Peter Sellers, Ian Carmichael, Terry-Thomas)

Saturday Night and Sunday Morning (1960)
Dir Karel Reisz (Albert Finney, Rachel Roberts, Shirley Anne Field)

School for Scoundrels (1960)
Dir Robert Hamer (Ian Carmichael, Alastair Sim, Terry-Thomas)

Village of the Damned (1960)
Dir Wolf Rilla (George Sanders, Barbara Shelley)

The Innocents (1961)
Dir Jack Clayton (Deborah Kerr, Michael Redgrave)

Dr No (1962)
Dir Terence Young (Sean Connery, Ursula Andress, Joseph Wiseman)

Lawrence of Arabia (1962)
Dir David Lean (Peter O'Toole, Omar Sharif, Alec Guinness)

The Loneliness of the Long Distance Runner (1962)
Dir Tony Richardson (Tom Courtenay, James Bolam, Julia Foster)

The Servant (1963)
Dir Joseph Losey (James Fox, Dirk Bogarde, Sarah Miles, Wendy Craig)

Billy Liar (1963)
Dir John Schlesinger (Tom Courtenay, Julie Christie, Wilfred Pickles)

This Sporting Life (1963)
Dir Lindsay Anderson (Richard Harris, Rachel Roberts)

Zulu (1964)
Dir Cy Endfield (Stanley Baker, Jack Hawkins, Michael Caine)

Culloden (1964)
Dir Peter Watkins (George McBean, Alan Pope, the people of Inverness)

Repulsion (1965)
Dir Roman Polanski (Catherine Deneuve, Yvonne Furneaux)

Blow-Up (1966)
Dir Michelangelo Antonioni (David Hemmings, Vanessa Redgrave, Paul Bowles)

Morgan – A Suitable Case For Treatment (1966)
Dir Karel Reisz (David Warner, Vanessa Redgrave, Robert Stephens)

The Devil Rides Out (1968)
Dir Terence Fisher (Christopher Lee, Charles Gray)

Oliver! (1968)
Dir Carol Reed (Ron Moody, Shani Wallis, Oliver Reed)

Witchfinder General (1968)
Dir Michael Reeves (Vincent Price, Patrick Wymark, Ian Ogilvy)

If... (1968)
Dir Lindsay Anderson (Malcom McDowell, David Wood, Richard Warwick)

Kes (1969)
Dir Ken Loach (David Bradley, Lynne Perrie, Freddie Fletcher)

The Railway Children (1970)
Dir Lionel Jeffries (Dinah Sheridan, William Mervyn, Jenny Agutter)

The Go Between (1970)
Dir Joseph Losey (Julie Christie, Alan Bates, Dominic Guard)

Deep End (1970)
Dir Jerzy Skolimowski (Jane Asher, John Moulder-Brown, Diana Dors)

Performance (1970)
Dirs Nicolas Roeg, Donald Cammell (James Fox, Mick Jagger, Anita Pallenberg)

Walkabout (1971)
Dir Nicolas Roeg (Jenny Agutter, David Gulpilil, Lucien John)

Get Carter (1971)
Dir Mike Hodges (Michael Caine, Britt Ekland, John Osborne)

The Offence (1972)
Dir Sidney Lumet (Sean Connery, Trevor Howard, Vivien Merchant)

The Bill Douglas Trilogy (1972, 1973, 1978)
Dir Bill Douglas (Stephen Archibald, Hughie Restorick)

The Ruling Class (1972)
Dir Peter Medak (Peter O'Toole, Alaister Sim, Coral Browne, Arthur Lowe)

Don't Look Now (1973)
Dir Nicolas Roeg (Julie Christie, Donald Sutherland)

The Wicker Man (1973)
Dir Robin Hardy (Edward Woodward, Christopher Lee, Britt Ekland)

Theatre of Blood (1973)
Dir Douglas Hickox (Vincent Price, Diana Rigg, Ian Hendry)

Edvard Munch (1974)
Dir Peter Watkins (Geir Westby, Gro Fraas, Iselin von Hanno Bart)

Monty Python and the Holy Grail (1974)
Dirs Terry Gilliam, Terry Jones (Graham Chapman, Michael Palin, John Cleese, Eric Idle et al)

Penda's Fen (1974)
Dir Alan Clarke (Spencer Banks, John Atkinson, Ian Hogg)

Nuts In May (1976)
Dir Mike Leigh (Roger Sloman, Alison Steadman)

Monty Python's Life of Brian (1979)
Dir Terry Jones (Graham Chapman, John Cleese, Michael Palin, Eric Idle)

The Long Good Friday (1980)
Dir John Mackenzie (Bob Hoskins, Helen Mirren, Derek Thompson)

Radio-On (1980)
Dir Chris Petit (David Beames, Lisa Kreuzer, Sandy Ratcliff)

Bad Timing (1980)
Dir Nicolas Roeg (Art Garfunkel, Theresa Russell, Harvey Keitel)

Sir Henry at Rawlinson End (1980)
Dir Steve Roberts (Trevor Howard, Patrick Magee)

Gregory's Girl (1981)
Dir Bill Forsyth (John Gordon Sinclair, Dee Hepburn, Claire Grogan)

Local Hero (1983)
Dir Bill Forsyth (Burt Lancaster, Peter Riegert, Denis Lawson)

Withnail and I (1987)
Dir Bruce Robinson (Richard E Grant, Paul McGann, Richard Griffiths)

The Long Day Closes (1992)
Dir Terence Davies (Marjorie Yates, Leigh McCormack, Anthony Watson)

Naked (1993)
Dir Mike Leigh (David Thewlis, Lesley Sharp, Karin Cartlidge)

Land and Freedom (1995)
Dir Ken Loach (Ian Hart, Icíar Bollaín, Tom Gilroy)

Trainspotting (1996)
Dir Danny Boyle (Ewan McGregor, Robert Carlyle, Jonny Lee Miller)

Gallivant (1996)
Dir Andrew Kötting (Andrew Kötting, Eden Kötting, Gladys Morris)

Secrets and Lies (1996)
Dir Mike Leigh (Brenda Blethyn, Timothy Spall, Marianne Jean-Baptiste)

Robinson in Space (1997)
Dir Patrick Keiller (Paul Scofield (voice))

Nil by Mouth (1997)
Dir Gary Oldman (Kathy Burke, Ray Winstone)

A Room for Romeo Brass (1999)
Dir Shane Meadows (Paddy Considine, Andrew Shim, Ben Marshall)

Wonderland (1999)
Dir Michael Winterbottom (Gina McKee, Shirley Henderson, Molly Parker, John Simm)

Topsy-Turvy (1999)
Dir Mike Leigh (Jim Broadbent, Allan Corduner, Timothy Spall)

In This World (2002)
Dir Michael Winterbottom (Jamal Udin Torabi, Enayatullah)
Dead Man's Shoes (2004)
Dir Shane Meadows (Paddy Considine, Gary Stretch, Toby Kebbell)

London to Brighton (2006)
Dir Paul Andrew Williams (Lorraine Stanley, Johnny Harris, Georgia Groome)

Kidulthood (2006)
Dir Menhaj Huda (Ami Ameen, Red Madrell, Noel Clarke)

This Is England (2006)
Dir Shane Meadows (Thomas Turgoose, Stephen Graham, Jo Hartley)

Adulthood (2008)
Dir Noel Clarke (Scarlett Alice Johnson, Adam Deacon)

Fish Tank (2009)
Dir Andrea Arnold (Katie Jarvis, Kierston Wareing, Michael Fassbender)

RECOMMENDED READING:

ICONS IN THE FIRE - The rise and fall of practically everyone in the British Film Industry 1984-2000. By Alexander Walker.

THE UNDECLARED WAR - The struggle for control of the World's film industry. By David Puttnam.

KILLER INSTINCT- How two young producers took on Hollywood and made the most controversial film of the decade. By Jane Hamsher.

BLADE RUNNERS, DEER HUNTERS AND BLOWING THE BLOODY DOORS OFF - My life in cult movies. By Michael Deeley.

100 FILMS AND A FUNERAL - The life and death of Polygram Films. By Michael Kuhn.

WILL WRITE AND DIRECT FOR FOOD. By Alan Parker.

KEN LOACH - The politics of film and television. By John Hill.

THE GOOD, THE BAD AND THE MULTIPLEX - What's wrong with modern movies? By Mark Kermode.

WHY ENGLAND SLEPT. By John F Kennedy.

SPIKE LEE - That's my story and I'm sticking to it. By Kaleem Aftab.

EASY RIDERS, RAGING BULLS - how the sex 'n' drugs 'n' rock 'n' roll generation saved Hollywood. By Peter Biskind.

A PORTRAIT OF THE ARTIST AS A POLITICAL DISSIDENT - The life and work of Aleksander Petrović. By Vlastimir Sudar.

FILM STYLE AND TECHNOLOGY: History and analysis. By Barry Salt.

THE UNDERGROUND FILM - An introduction to its development in America. By Sheldon Renan.

MY INDECISION IS FINAL - The Spectacular Rise and Fall of Goldcrest Films, the Independent Studio That Challenged Hollywood. By Jake Eberts and Terry Ilott.

ABOUT THE AUTHORS.

Vinod Mahindru, was born in 1969, in Birmingham, the youngest of three children.

His father was born in the Punjab region of India. His mother, also born in India, grew up in Tanzania. They both came to the UK in the early 1960's where his father worked at the General Post Office, while his mother had children, did a teacher training course, and then worked as a schoolteacher.

In 1986, Vinod studied at *Matthew Boulton College* where he made his first short film on VHS video. In 1988, he did a City & Guilds course in TV and Audio Production at *Sandwell College of Further Education*, gaining a distinction in Media Studies. He then studied photography at *The Birmingham Institute of Art and Design* before gaining a place at the *London Film School* in 1991, where he graduated with a diploma in 'The Art and Technique of Film Making.'

His short films include: *The Fruit Pastilles* (1987), *Pleasure Beach* (1989), *Unisex* (1991), *To Get Rich is Glorious* (1998). *Our Father* (2000), *In Broad Daylight* (2002), and *Red Faces* (2002).

He lives in Birmingham, England, where, until September 2017, he worked as a cinema supervisor for Cineworld Cinemas.

With Robin Dutta, he produced and directed the documentary film, *Who Killed British Cinema?*

Jonathan Gems is a playwright and screenwriter whose plays include: *The Tax Exile, Naked Robots, The Paranormalist*, and *Susan's Breasts*. His films include *1984, White Mischief, Mars Attacks!* and *The Treat*, which he also directed.

Index

THE DOCUMENTARY THE

Ben Kingsley   Ken Loach
Stephen Frears   Alan

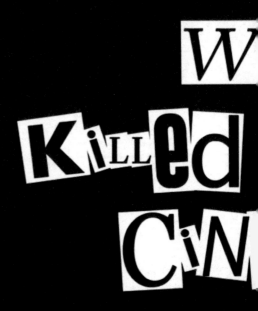

PRODUCED & DIRECTED

AUDE ACCARY-BONNERY - SAM BERN - JONATHAN GEMS - STEFAN GEORGIOU -
SCOTT JOHNSTON - GERALD KAUFMAN - PAT KAUFMAN - TONY KLINGER - MICHA
NEIL OSEMAN - MICHEL PLAZANET - JON ROSLING - ELIZABETH RYMER - ROGER SHA

 @QuotaFilms   #whoKill

www.WhoKilled

WHO KILLED

BRITISH CINEMA?

SEE THE FILM!

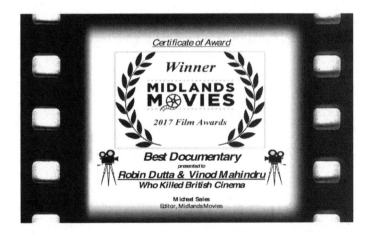

The real UK film industry.

Your films, Your culture.

The truth about your film career in Britain!